Perfect Moments in Relationships

Lessons in Connection for Work, Family, Love, and Life

By Brian R. King LCSW

Published by Brian R. King International

ISBN: 978-0-9896948-1-0

Dedication

To my family: you are my heart, which makes you something I could never live without.

Special Thanks:

Shannon Bush (http://creativepossibility.com.au), for her amazing cover design of this book, as well as her wonderful feedback on its contents.

Linda Weaver, for her meticulous and thorough editing of this book. You are a kind and patient professional. You can learn more about Linda's other areas of brilliance at http://www.tutorbasket.com.

Suzie Lake (www.ELCATutoring.com), for creating many of the discussion questions provided at the end of this book.

Tammy Whitten (www.womenmanagingstress.com), for suggesting the addition of discussion questions to help people take the lessons in this book even further, and for creating many of them herself.

Lauren Young, of Freshly Baked Communications (Marketing@FBC-Chicago.com) and Jennifer DiBella, of the Hot Cakes Group (hello@hotcakesgroup.com), for their brilliant recommendations for organizing the contents of this book, as well as their tireless efforts in helping it reach as many people as possible.

Table of Contents

Preface

"Perfect doesn't mean flawless. Perfect means it does exactly what I need it to do."—Seth Godin

Relationships can be more difficult to navigate than the ocean at night during a hurricane. Now try doing it with touches of Autism, ADHD, Dyslexia and other challenges. This has been my struggle, but also my greatest gift.

I need to work harder than most to discover and experience those perfect moments—the moments when things feel like they're working together. The most special moments are the ones in which I have effectively connected with another human being and we both became better as a result. Those perfect moments are the subject of this book and the greatest treasure of life, as far as I'm concerned.

My unique situation has required me to look more deeply at myself and at the nature of what it means to connect to another human being. Living with a mind that is racing, scattered, and often confused in fast-paced social environments, has required me to become resourceful in a way few "typical" people will ever need to be. I am eternally grateful for this.

What my life has become as a result of this journey is one in which I can show others from all walks of life how to navigate the noise of their own minds, lives, and relationships, in order to truly connect with one another.

You don't need to have experienced the challenges I have in order to benefit from the lessons I've learned. I'm mentioning my challenges here simply to offer you some context on what gave rise to my experiences and ideas.

It also explains why this book is organized the way it is. One of the unique quirks of my brain is that I often remember my life out of order. It's like a box of photographs without dates to tell when certain events happened, so that I can place them in the proper order.

It also makes it difficult to connect the experiences of my life into a cohesive story. So, what I've learned to do is capture moments, the individual lessons, and extract from them everything I can.

In your hands, here, you have a box of photographs. You have a collection of teachable moments from my life, from my ongoing experiments with communication and connection.

There's no need to read this book as though one moment is designed to flow into the next. It often doesn't and it doesn't need to.

I suggest you simply enjoy a lesson and contemplate it for a while. Consider what action, if any, you can take from it, and then move on.

I've also chosen to format the text in a way that allows people like me to read and comprehend it more efficiently.

Treat this box of snapshots, not as a roadmap or a blueprint, on how to have successful relationships. Think of it more as a box of Legos. There are many pieces that can be assembled in a variety of ways, depending on what you want to create. Try to put a few pieces together, and if you don't like what you've created take them apart and try something else. Make sense?

I apologize in advance to the "Grammar Police" and members of the Royal Order of Form and Function, who may spontaneously break out in hives as they navigate a field of occasional run-on sentences and frequent fragments.

I offer these not to confuse or offend people but as part of my ongoing investigation of the rules of written and verbal communication that so many of us have been raised to believe are gospel truth. Rules that in the end have resulted in communication that's as complicated and fraught with misunderstandings as ever.

You will find that many of these observations aren't strategies *per se* as much as they are opportunities for reflection that when understood create an opportunity for you to approach others more consciously than ever before.

Many of the beliefs and strategies I'll offer you may feel counterintuitive. But that makes sense, doesn't it? You intuit the approach you were raised with and I'll be holding up many of those popular beliefs about communication to intense scrutiny.

Your ultimate success in applying what you'll discover in these pages is based on following a willing partner who is sick of the status quo of modern communication norms that are riddled with cues, signals, innuendo, and expectations of mind-reading that typically result in hurt feelings and broken trust. None of which had to happen, but continues to, day after day, because those involved don't know what to do instead. Until now. Ready to dig in? Let's go.

Life

The 4 R's of life

KISS – Keep it simple, Student.

What is your life built on? What do you stand for? Where is your life headed?

A prevailing principle of my life is simplify, simplify, simplify. There is no better place to practice that rule than when it comes to relationships. All of my communication, and in fact all of my life, has become about growing in four key areas, what I refer to as the 4 core competencies of life, or the 4 R's.

I imagine you could think of more, but I hope that as you explore these, you'll realize that they're both simple and comprehensive in how they capture the essence of what is most important as we create the life and relationships we truly want.

They're not the same as the Four R's taught in school, which are Read, Remember, Regurgitate and Repeat. The Four R's that I'm referring to are Responsibility, Resourcefulness, Resilience, and Reciprocity.

As you'll see, the R's are not mutually exclusive but are branches of the same tree. It's difficult to discuss one without reference to another. You will see each of the 4R's repeated throughout the book in varying ways and the overlap will be apparent.

That's another reason why trying to divide this book logically into chapters would have been next to impossible. It would be like trying to separate the clouds from the sky. They flow in and out of each other more so than building upon one another.

Responsibility

"There are two primary choices in life: to accept conditions as they exist, or accept the responsibility for changing them."
—*Denis Waitley*

What does responsibility mean? It doesn't mean accepting blame.

Responsibility means accepting complete ownership of your life and its direction. It means a decision to be proactive, to take steps, to take action, to create things, not to sit around and wait for them to happen, not to wait for them to come to you.

Responsibility means you own everything happening between your ears, whether there are misfiring circuits or not. You don't blame your challenges, you don't blame the world... you don't blame anything or anyone.

When you move from blame to responsibility, you move from a life that happens to you to a life that you create. You're able to take action in ways that you never thought possible. You're able to see the fruits of your own labor and more importantly, you're able to see all of the gifts you've locked away for so long now begin to take root out in the world and other people's lives.

Instead of hiding behind blame, excuses, and procrastination, you're actually putting seeds out in the world and watching things blossom simply because your responsible presence on this earth actually adds value and makes a difference.

When I fully embraced this, I felt things begin to shift in my life very quickly. I mean, within days. When a flood of new opportunity comes into your life, you also sense a new level of responsibility you didn't have before and it can feel overwhelming.

In the past, I would sabotage that success out of fear that I couldn't handle it or wasn't worth it. But now I realize what I am doing, so I spend time reflecting until I discover a way to be excited about the opportunity instead of intimidated.

What I began doing instead was telling myself that an opportunity that required more responsibility than I've ever had before was something for me to step into.

I now ask myself, "Who's the person I need to become to step into this new level of responsibility?"

3

I remind myself that I planted the seed to create this opportunity. The seed grew into this chance, so I need to grow to meet it.

One thing that can help in these situations, as well, is learning how to transform fear into excitement.

When you examine both fear and excitement on a physical level, they actually feel the same way. You feel tension in your abdomen; you feel tension in your shoulders. Your breathing gets a little bit faster. Perhaps you feel butterflies in your stomach. You start to sweat.

The same physical responses are made different by the story you tell yourself about what those feelings mean. If you say, "I'm starting to sweat. My pulse is racing. My stomach's tightening up. That must mean danger's coming."

If you say instead, "My stomach is tightening up. I'm sweating. My pulse is racing. All right, I'm ready to jump in there and make something happen. I'm ready to take action now."

Your conclusion makes all the difference.

Resourcefulness

"Remember you will not always win. Some days, the most resourceful individual will taste defeat. But there is, in this case, always tomorrow - after you have done your best to achieve success today."— *Maxwell Maltz*

Resources exist in three forms; people, places, and things. We live in a family, a community, a society. Our number one resource in this life is each other. We were not put on this planet to go it alone.

There are times when we allow others to lean on us and times when we must do the leaning. There is a myth in this world that it's weak to ask for help. I've worked with clients over the years that say, "My friends don't ask for help. I shouldn't have to either." I look at them stunned and say, "What makes you think they don't ask for help?"

"Because I never see them do it."

My question then is, "Do you ever see them take a shower? No? Is it reasonable to say they do it? Maybe some not as often as they should, but you know they do it."

It's a fool who believes he does everything alone.

What places can you go to that are resources to you? You may visit the doctor's office, grocery store, or maybe a park when you just want to relax.

Then there are things. Your favorite song that always energizes you, a cold glass of wine after a long day. Things can also be knowledge, your favorite book or quote.

Maybe a thing can also be a pencil that you fidget with to help you think. It can be the Internet that helps you find the answers you so desperately need. Resources constantly surround us and some of them are invisible to us.

Do you drive a car? Then the car is not your only resource. The people who were involved in assembling it so you could use it are resources to you. You are connected to everybody who was in that chain of events.

For example, the gas that fuels your car began with people you'll likely never meet who pumped the oil out of the ground, refined it, shipped it, and brought it to your local gas station, then charged you too much for it. They are all resources to you.

Many people are oblivious to the abundance of resources in their lives because they don't practice strategic thinking. Strategic thinking is about deliberately creating things in your life—having a sense of where you're headed, so that when the resources needed present themselves, you can spot them more easily.

Living deliberately also helps you become more proficient at sorting out the resources you can use from the impulsive whims that show up on a daily basis.

The reality is that there are far fewer things that really need our attention in life and the rest can be allowed to float right by.

Life is only as simple as your focus is.

One more thought I have on this is how frequently people fail to take a thorough inventory of just how many useful qualities they have. People may so closely associate with their profession, their hobby, their role as a parent, and are so used to doing the skills that make them effective in those areas that they lose sight of the vast number of resources they actually possess.

One of the greatest compliments I ever received was from a former teacher who once observed me presenting and said, "What most amazes me about you is that you use all of yourself."

I've discovered that the one category that allows me to be mindful of everything I have to offer is "human being." That term includes everything about me—my spirituality, my confidence as well as my vulnerability, what I do as a father, counselor, writer, presenter, husband, you name it.

The more conscious I am of all of my resources, especially within myself, the more resourceful I can be, more often and more quickly.

Resilience

"Life is not about how fast you run, or how high you climb, but how well you bounce."—Unknown

Resilience is the art of getting up instead of giving up. It's about bouncing back and weathering whatever storm that life sends your way.

In fact, when you consider the age you're at now, you must acknowledge that every single day of your life you got up and whatever happened to you, you got through it somehow. Then you got up the next morning and you kept going.

There are so many people I've come across who said, "I can't do it. It's too much. It's overwhelming. I don't know what to do." Really? Your history contradicts that statement.

Your history tells you that every single day you've gotten up and you've kicked butt in some way. You found a way to make it work. You took responsibility for getting through that day.

You somehow found the resources to allow you to solve those problems, or at least hang on, because maybe that problem is going to get solved today, maybe it'll be tomorrow or the next week.

You at least found the resources to hang on and you kept going. You bounced back.

I am a 25-year cancer survivor. Stage 3 testicular cancer was my graduation present from high school. It was without question the worst summer of my life. The physical pain, the losing of my hair, the losing of my friends, the losing of my girlfriend—the complete unraveling of life, as I knew it. My peers just couldn't handle that situation. So they kept their distance.

My family and I didn't have a good support system, nor were we good at supporting each other. So I was pretty much left trying to figure it out and feeling like the world had turned its back on me.

I became angry, bitter, disappointed, disgusted... every negative emotion you could imagine. But when I eventually learned that my cancer was in remission, and that I would live, I made the decision then and there that not only was I not going to live it negatively, but I refused to allow myself to ever feel that helpless again.

So I committed myself to learning whatever it is I needed to, to lead a solution-focused life, to become more resourceful and resilient.

From then on, any challenge that life threw at me reminded me of the belief that I don't "do" helpless. Though some of those challenges knocked me down for a while, I was committed to finding a way.

When I couldn't find the answer in books, I realized that there had to be somebody else out there that had gone through this before. I'm not so special that I'm the first one this has ever happened to.

But it's pretty easy to feel alone when it's the first time it's ever happened to you; it's a unique experience. You have no point of reference. You don't necessarily have the skill- set for it.

In these moments it's important to realize that this is your first day at school. You are a student again and you need to find a teacher. These situations give you an opportunity to learn, develop, and refine a skill that you haven't had to use yet.

Those who have succeeded before us have left little clues to how they did it... beliefs or actions that are duplicatable. Become the person that you need to be to implement that skill.

Every fall, every adversity refines you. Whether it's cancer, divorce, bankruptcy, or just falling and skinning your knee. That's part of the grand adventure we call the human experience.

Somebody out there has an answer for you. Find that person.

All of this time and effort isn't just for you. When you refine yourself, everyone benefits—your family, your friends (whoever that is).

I have a brain that moves at the speed of a Ferrari at times and patience can be very elusive. Yet the process of bouncing back can require the patience of a gardener who realizes that certain things need to be nurtured over time.

So if I want to create something that takes time, I cannot resign myself to believing I'm just an inpatient person. I need to find a place in myself that can be paced. A place where I can grasp the steering wheel of my Ferrari brain and have greater say in its speed and direction. Otherwise certain goals are just not going to be within my reach.

The lack of willingness and commitment to develop qualities like patience, honesty, or integrity, can separate you from where you are now to where you want to be.

It's that simple determination to learn what I need to know to escape helplessness that compels me to keep pulling myself up again. It's always with help in some form from someone. That's been the story of my life, getting knocked down and getting back up.

I imagine your story is different only in the details.

Reciprocity

"My strengths are the reason you need me and my challenges are the reason I need you."—Brian R. King

In my experience, independence is a myth, because when you look at the definition of independence it means "to do without help".

How on earth can we possibly succeed without help? I am not speaking to you right now independent of this book. I did not get where I am independent of those who taught me to read, write, drive etc.

11

I don't achieve anything in my life independent of the people in my life. Success does not occur in a vacuum, it occurs in a context.

It occurs in a relationship, in a family, in a classroom, in a workplace, or in a community. We cannot do it alone. We were not meant to do it alone. We are in it together and we must be in it together. That's the only way we're going to make it.

In fact, here's a principle I realized that explains perfectly that being here for each other is a rule of life. I call it the rule of reciprocity. It states that my strengths are the reason you need me and my challenges are the reason I need you.

We're here to complement each other, to balance each other out, to create that unique synergy that can only happen when we come together and utilize each other's strengths to connect with one another and help each other grow.

For the purpose of this book, it is critical for you to remember this. You are a partner in every moment you spend with another person. Every moment in which you interact with another human being, you're partnering with that person to co-create that moment.

In that moment you have a sacred opportunity to create a shared experience. The goal isn't to be perfect though we may occasionally experience what we might call perfect moments, the goal is to as often as possible be mindful, present and deliberate in what we bring to that moment with our partner.

Though I'm not present with you physically, my thoughts on these pages allow me to partner with you right now. You and I are partners in creating this experience together. You and I are taking this journey together.

Time to be Polite

"Always give a word or sign of salute when meeting or passing a friend, or even a stranger, if in a lonely place."—Tecumseh

It's polite to hold the door open for others, right?

That's why you do things like that, right?

Is that all there is to it, being polite?

Is this rote behavior done for no other reason than the blind acceptance of another social protocol: Was this part of the socialization process that has led you to become the successful person that you are?

I used to argue against social conventions especially when the reasons I was given to follow them were. "Because that's how it's done," "Because it's polite" etc.

This all changed for me several years ago when I was carrying a heavy box toward the entrance of a building where I had an office. A person entered the building well ahead of me and could have easily carried on but instead she chose to wait.

She held the door wide open for me so I could walk through easily. I thanked her and she said, "I saw you coming and thought it would be hard for you to open the door."

That was the key for me as to why it is so critical as fellow human beings that we take the time to offer these simple gestures to each other and use them as a means to truly see each other.

Also, to realize that we are all in this together and need to take the time to remind each other with these simple gestures that we aren't invisible and that we all matter.

The next time you hold a door for a stranger or offer any other polite gesture, do it with the spirit of I SEE YOU and see how it feels.

In that moment, it ceases to be a social convention and becomes a moment in which you connected with another person.

What's Your Truth?

"Everything we hear is an opinion, not a fact. Everything we see is a perspective, not the truth."—Marcus Aurelius

Many years ago I had a colleague who was very fond of the phrase, "Well, that's your truth."

Ironically, she found it particularly useful when mistreating her colleagues.

She was a very intelligent woman with much to teach, but her approach to others created resentment instead of respect. Especially when others would "call" her on her treatment of them and she'd respond with, "Well, that's your truth."

She seemed to never take responsibility for her actions toward others and put everything on them.

Keep in mind—I advocate the absolute necessity for each of us to take 100% responsibility for our responses to the events and people in our lives.

I also advocate that we take 100% responsibility for what we put out into the world and into the lives of others.

Allow me to offer a tweak to the idea that we each have our own truth.

As people, we don't know "jack" about "truth", but we're loaded with our own perceptions that refine our lens on the world.

Our perceptions are based on the decisions we've made about how the world works, and they are really the best we can do, and that's all right. As long as we realize that's what we're doing.

More important to realize is that's what everyone else is doing as well.

Each of us walks through each day of our lives telling ourselves a story about the way the world works. Sometimes we tell stories similar enough to others that when we meet them we feel connected. We have experiences of "Me too."

Yet, we meet others with different stories and openly criticize them for being "wrong", "stupid", "unpatriotic"...take your pick.

The reality is that none of us has a truth (regardless of a tendency to self-appoint as designated truth-bearer of the universe). But we each do have our own story—a very real and compelling story that determines the obstacles we believe exist and the opportunities we believe are available to us.

As we raise our children, or manage our subordinates, we develop a story about who they are and what we decide they can and can't do. With enough repetition they begin to accept our story about them as their own. Make sure the story contains more opportunities than obstacles.

Well that's my story and I'm sticking to it. That is, until I'm no longer satisfied with the results it's giving me, then I'll rewrite the story so I can have a better ending.

The Curse of the Calendar

"We must not allow the clock and the calendar to blind us to the fact that each moment of life is a miracle and mystery."—*H. G. Wells*

It never ceases to amaze me that so many people rely upon the calendar to determine their emotional states.

On social media I see the weekly gripefest from those who have decided that Monday is designed to ruin their lives in various ways.

These people also celebrate "Hump Day" in the middle of the week as they experience the mid-point of their self-imposed treacherous climb up a mountain of daily life.

Friday, of course, is the day they feel they've been paroled from the drudgery of gainful employment to a two-day furlough after which they are wrongfully returned to Monday.

I'm not minimizing the difficulties of any one's life here, I am making the very important distinction between genuine challenges and the completely irrational belief that the day of the week has some overwhelming power to determine the quality of your life.

I have no interest in telling you how to live your life any more than I want your advice on how to part my hair (I'm bald by the way). I only seek to offer suggestions based on the many options I've discovered. Let's explore some of the options you have:

Motivation or Monotony

Is energy given to you or taken from you? A more important question is, are you energized, excited, lit-up? If not, why not?

"What you seek so shall you find." Once you've determined your day is going to suck, your mind has this stubborn need to be right. You will then seek out any and all evidence to support your original hypothesis that Mondays suck and you will then end your day by jumping on your favorite social media outlet to share your findings and prove once again that you are particularly skilled in the area of the self-fulfilling prophecy.

If you're going to be motivated to prove anything, prove that you can make it a *great* day instead of simply proving that you're capable of remaining in a rut.

Outcomes or Oh no!'s

What experiences do you want to have today? One of my clients has really embraced the importance of shaping his family life according to the outcomes he wants to experience. So much so that he's made asking the following question of his family members a standard practice, "What are you going to do to make it a great day?"

This simple question reminds each of them that they can be personally responsible, proactive, focused and create their experiences instead of simply sitting back and passively waiting for life to happen.

Next or No Fairs

What's next? A single event doesn't define the quality of your day. So often one of my kids will come home from school and say he had a bad day. Upon further examination what typically happened was that one or two things happened that he didn't like and he chose to fixate on it and miss any opportunity to move past it.

I've also met many people who don't learn from their experience because they don't believe there's a lesson in their experiences. They instead act as though they simply have a series of random events in their lives that have no purpose other than to inconvenience or punish them.

Discovery or Dissatisfaction

Are you celebrating everything that's wrong with your life or cursing everything that isn't good enough? I'm not a sports fan and I'm grateful, because when I read posts from people who say that their life will be over if their favorite football team doesn't win a game then I really have to prioritize to keep these people out of my circle of influence.

I implore you to examine whether these events truly deserve the importance you give them. Does it really make sense to hang your emotional health on an outcome in which you have absolutely no say?

Attention or Avoidance

Where's your focus? Do you spend your day alert, aware, and engaged, or hopelessly tuned out just trying to get through it. Life is for living, not for surviving.

YES or Yikes!

Move into your day with enthusiasm instead of dread. Realize that you are stepping out into a world that provides more than the "same shit different day". It provides a day where every moment, every thought, and every action can move things in a whole new direction.

How will you make it a great day?

Feedback is the oxygen of Relationships

"Let every eye negotiate for itself and trust no agent."—William Shakespeare

A fundamental misunderstanding in life is that relationships are simply the way they are, that there are generalized rules that always occur in every relationship, and if you learn them, you'll be okay, right?

I don't have to tell you just how wrong that is. The reality is that you have the right to negotiate the relationships in your life.

You have the right to negotiate each relationship in your life. Establish the dos and don'ts—the things that better happen in the relationship and the things that must never happen, ultimately arriving at a relationship that will work for both of you.

The best way to establish these parameters is through clear, consistent feedback. So, let's discuss how to make sure we get it in a way that builds you up and moves you forward.

For strong and stable partnerships, there are three main things that you need to negotiate with your partner, whether it is your child, spouse, or colleague:

1. You agree that you are going to give each other feedback on what is and is not working in your partnership.

In my case, I know that I miss a lot of visual social cues. I also know I can ramble on and on if I get really excited about a topic—and I know sometimes that can be overwhelming for others, so I want feedback when I am doing this and do not notice.

In my relationship with my wife Cathy, for instance, I will ask her for feedback on that specific tendency—when I am talking too much, I would like to know that she would like a turn or has spotted that somebody else would like a turn talking and I haven't noticed it.

2. You will agree exactly how to give each other feedback.

I want feedback but I want it in such a way that I don't feel like I was just punched in the gut. It is easier to hear feedback and use it when it is supportive instead of critical. Therefore, I negotiate how to give me that feedback.

I can negotiate an obvious hand signal that Cathy and I have agreed to. I can negotiate her saying something very gentle to me such as, "Excuse me, I would like to add something here." That is how she lets me know, and because we negotiated that phrase, I know that phrase means specifically this, "Hey, Brian, you have been talking too long, you need to pause and let someone else contribute."

The spoken word is critical here in relating to me because I am so auditory. I had a client with a tendency to get louder as he talked, so we negotiated between he and his siblings that they would use a hand signal to cue him to lower his voice. He was more visual and shared that a hand signal would be more effective for him.

The signal was subtle and allowed him to get the feedback he needed to adjust without feeling like he has been "outed" or criticized in front of everybody in the room. That is why it is important to negotiate both what to give feedback on and specifically how to give it.

3. You agree to how you will receive the feedback.

This is a very important point. Some people will say, "Be honest with me," and when you are, they get mad. Why would you want to give feedback to a person who will only get angry with you? Negotiating this third step is where you solve that problem.

In Step 1, you negotiate precisely what you want to receive feedback on. In Step 2, you determine how to give feedback so you know it when you're getting it; in the way you're able to accept it. After negotiating all that, why would you get angry?

If a person is giving you what you asked for in the way you asked for it, there is no reason to be angry. Instead, you negotiate to receive the feedback with gratitude, not anger.

Then the first time a person does give you feedback in the agreed-upon way, and you do respond the way you agreed to, guess what you are going to get? Trust, because you kept your end of the agreement. Then you'll get more feedback, more clarification, and more opportunities to improve your relationship.

A great question to agree to receive feedback on regularly is "What about our relationship would you like to see working better for you?"

Stay away from questions such as "What's wrong with our relationship?" "Is there anything missing?" The use of deficit language causes us to become guarded instead of receptive.

Another variation could be, "What about our relationship can be working even better for you?" The foundation of that question being that there are things already working well to be built on for even better results.

Stop Pushing my Buttons!

"Between stimulus and response, man has the freedom to choose."—Victor Frankl

Do some people really push your buttons?

This expression refers to the seemingly magical ability of others to say or do just the right thing to upset you.

Here's the question: who installed those buttons in the first place? They didn't. You did, and they simply discovered them.

Solution: remove the button. How?

A button is essentially an emotionally charged belief about what shouldn't occur in life (as far as your comfort zone is concerned) and a decision about how you must respond when it does.

Over time, you tend to lose your awareness of this pattern, as it becomes habit and the process hardwires itself into your nervous system so you can pay less attention to it.

The more reactive you are, the more buttons you have. Make sense?

Being upset or offended is a two-step process:

1. You decide an event (a phrase, a person etc.) is unacceptable

2. You decide that when it occurs you MUST announce your displeasure with a strong, emotional response. (I'm

not talking about pitching a fit; by *strong* I mean it disrupts whatever you were feeling with intense upset in some way).

Here's a simple formula for removing a button:

E + R = O (Event + Response = Outcome)

As with any math problem, you change one of the variables and you change the result. In this case, the one variable you have the most influence over is your response—your belief about how you MUST respond.

So many of life's frustrations are the direct result of decisions to make things that really don't concern you into things worthy of your undivided attention and your upset.

Questions to ask yourself:

Is this event really worthy of the meaning I assign to it?
Is it really worthy of the attention I give it?
Is it really worthy of my focus at the expense of something else I could be giving my attention to?
I encourage you to do a thorough "button" evaluation and consider a complete button overhaul.

You'll be amazed by how many buttons you've installed and even more amazed at how much less stressful life will become once they're gone.

What do you replace these buttons with? The conscious awareness to choose how to respond to the events of your life.

If your past is Lousy, Perhaps the Problem is your Memory

"There are lots of people who mistake their imagination for their memory."—Josh Billings

So what do we know about the past? Do we remember what happened—what *really* happened? Do we only remember the meaning we assigned to the events we remember?

You and I have memories of what went right and what went wrong in our lives but seldom do we take the time to examine just how biased our versions of things/events truly are. We then allow that bias to rob us of joy for years, and at worst for life, simply because we chose to decide through the eyes of our side alone.

With that, how in the heck do you create a past worth remembering? Do you shove all that negativity into the back of your mind like it never happened? Do you try to force yourself to believe useless pleasantries like, "It's all for the best," or "Someday you'll be able to look back at this and laugh?" I'm sure you have a few you could share as well. Of course you don't do that—denial is no solution. It doesn't change the past and it certainly will never improve upon it.

As I mentioned earlier, one way you and I kick our own butts, when it comes to the past, is the mistaken belief that we have "immaculate perception". That's the belief that we got it right the first time. "I don't need to clarify. I know what you meant, I heard what you said," and other lies that we use to deny ourselves the opportunity to get more information, to get a clearer picture of things. A few years ago I learned a valuable lesson about just how inaccurate my own memory is.

It happened when a good friend dragged me (metaphorically) to my 20th high school reunion. I was in the process of a divorce and my self-esteem was at one of the lowest points it has ever been.

I went there telling myself that none of these people cared about me, most of them had never said a word to me, and I didn't have anything that would interest them anyway. This is what happened next.

I walked into the hall where the reunion was taking place and I was in the room maybe two minutes when a former classmate named Allison approached me with a big smile. She gave me a big hug and said, "Hi! I'm so glad you made it, how have you been?"

Allison was one of the prettiest girls in school and never said a word to me the whole time. She wasn't mean to me—we had several classes together but she never talked to me. For the record, I didn't make an effort to talk to her either.

I was surprised by her enthusiasm and figured she thought I was somebody else, so I asked, "Do you know who I am?" She said, "Of course I do, you're Brian King." I felt completely disoriented by this and had to figure out what was going on.

I said, "Wait a minute. We never said a word to each other all through high school, so why are you happy to see me?" This is the part that caused me to rethink my entire memory of high school. She said, "I always thought you were a really cool guy. I just never knew how to approach you."

That was a HOLY COW moment of galactic proportions. She and I talked about this a while longer and it was revealed that it was my eccentricities that did not in fact turn her and possibly others off about me. What they did was make it difficult for others to find a common point of reference to use as a basis to start a conversation with me. So it's possible I had many people who wanted to befriend me and had no idea how to do so.

I thanked Allison for sharing that with me and told her how much it meant to me that she did. She single-handedly helped me rewrite a painful part of my past through the realization that my memories were based on too little information about why things happened as they did.

The rest of the evening was punctuated by similar reactions from people who were eager to hear about my life as they shared positive memories of me from high school. I was equally excited to learn where their lives have taken them. I had no idea my classmates remembered me so positively. They didn't say anything back then. Again, I also didn't ask.

What I did do was to draw the ridiculous conclusion that I wasn't liked. I followed the doctrine that no news is bad news. Are you getting my point here?

Our memories of the things that were missing in life are typically incomplete, as I discovered. But once I learned more, from a perspective other than my own, my experience became so much fuller.

So my question to you for this moment is simple. Which memory are you going to improve upon first?

Can you Repeat That?

"If you don't say anything, you won't be called on to repeat it."
—Calvin Coolidge

Negotiating to clarify, as I mentioned earlier, is critical. People who respond with statements such as, "You should've been listening," "I don't want to repeat myself," are treating a request to repeat something as disrespectful, when, in reality, all their colleague wants is to make sure she got it right.

With my clients, I will ask if he understood what I said. When he says he did, I ask them to repeat it. In fact, quite often he apologizes, because he may have spaced out for a moment or was processing something I previously said and missed what I had just said.

He tuned out for a second, and who doesn't? You can't pay attention a hundred percent of the time. Paying attention can be especially difficult we frequently check out. Reducing these misunderstandings requires us to be honest about these moments instead of faking understanding.

With friends, family and clients, I negotiate for the right to ask me to repeat myself if they do not hear something I said, because I know, then, that it is important enough to them that they want me to repeat it.

You are a Hero

"Hard times don't create heroes. It is during the hard times when the 'hero' within us is revealed."—Bob Riley

Do you consider yourself a hero? By the time you're done reading this perhaps you'll feel differently.

What makes somebody a hero? Is it because s/he committed a grand act of courage that landed them on the nightly news? Is it because s/he won an award or was written about in the newspaper for the work s/he does?

No, in my experience what makes you or anyone else a hero is one simple act of compassion towards another human being in need.

I was raised back in the 70's and 80's when words like Autism Spectrum and ADHD did not exist but described my experience fully.

I struggled all through school being bullied by peers and teachers alike, being laughed at, excluded, treated horribly, struggling, not knowing why I couldn't make the world work.

I also had Dyslexia and didn't know it. I had all the reasons in the world to give up and a couple of times, I considered it. But I didn't. I kept going.

What helped me keep going?

On occasion, through all those struggles, somebody would show up with a simple act of compassion, someone who saw the little weird kid sitting off to the side of the playground being left out, someone who saw me and said "That kid matters and I'm going to let him know it."

There are three things that every hero does: they have a belief, they make a decision, and they take action. That's how they make an impact in the lives of others.

Every time you believe in somebody else—when you believe that they matter —and you decide to take action and let them know it, you, in that moment, are the hero that person was waiting for. Maybe it's a colleague. Maybe it's a relative who is struggling.

You show up right when you are needed, to let them know in that moment of adversity they are not alone. That's what makes you a hero.

My graduation present from high school was stage three testicular cancer. The friends I did have couldn't handle it, so they kept their distance. They stopped talking to me.

I remember all those weeks in the hospital alone with TV and a few books. Then one day, I broke down in tears because it all became too much.

At that moment the nurse walked in, right when I needed her. She sat down next to me on my hospital bed and held my hand as I cried. She didn't say anything. She was just there.

She listened as I talked about how hard it was, why me, why did this have to happen? She didn't say anything but she was there and she cared. She was there when I needed her and that made her a hero to me.

A powerful principle she practiced in that moment is that you can never say the wrong thing while listening. She was there, she cared, and she was my hero.

I was told after I went into remission for cancer that I would likely never have children. Today I am privileged to be the father of three boys.

It turns out that my children also inherited the variety of the Autism Spectrum that I had when I was a child. I discovered this about myself through them. When they entered the school system they struggled every single day to make the world work.

I needed to show them how to make the world work. They have come so far over these years because, instead of giving up, I decided to stand up and be the hero they needed. I needed to be their model of perseverance.

What is perseverance after all? It is the art of getting up instead of giving up.

My life story is punctuated with plenty of opportunities where I could have stayed down but I got back up. Why? Because a hero stepped in who believed in me, decided to let me know it, and helped me discover in myself that I was worth fighting for.

My heroes reminded me that I just needed to take one more step, just one more day. Give life one more chance. It will get better.

Those were lessons that I paid forward and continue to pay forward to my three boys, my wife, and my friends.

My boys don't struggle as much as they once did because they have learned those powerful lessons.

I don't care how thick that wall seems, I don't care how heavy that burden feels, just one more step, one more chance, one more day.

It always works out, but you must keep going.

My boys are my heroes because I see how much they have accomplished. I see how they were once afraid of life but are now eager to experience it. How excited they are about what tomorrow brings because they have learned just one more step, just one more day. It always gets better. It always works out.

I have no doubt that you have done that for someone else or someone has done that for you. You have seen another person when s/he was down. You reached your hand out and you said, "You are not alone. We are in this together. Just have one more moment and one more day. We'll get through this."

Now I ask you this question again. Do you think you are a hero? I hope you do. I want to personally thank you for being who you are. Thank you for the contribution that you make in the lives of your fellow human beings each and every day because we need more heroes in this world, more people that see each other. Believe in each other.

Make the decision to take action and help make the world a better place. The biggest gift as a hero you give the rest of the world is because somebody else is watching you to see how it's done.

To observe in real time the art of getting up instead of giving up is a part of your great legacy to the people around you.

To show them how to keep going for one more day, take one more chance, because that is all it takes to find a better tomorrow.

I Want A Normal Life!

"Normal is not something to aspire to; it's something to get away from."—Jodie Foster

I frequently receive emails from people who are experiencing struggles in relationships and express that they just want to be normal and have normal relationships.

Normal?

When I ask them what they mean by "normal" they say things like "I want to be like everyone else", "I want to fit in", "I want to be happy".

It's the "I want to be happy," that really gets the conversation going. When I ask what will make them happy they say things like "I want to be accepted for who I am", "I want people to see that I have something to offer". This is a significant shift from wanting to be like everyone else.

Wanting to be accepted for who you are is a desire for respect, significance, and individuality; it isn't about wanting to blend in. It is about wanting to stand out but in a way that doesn't result primarily in criticism.

Wanting a "normal" life in its literal sense is aspiring to something typical, average. When examined more closely, this desire for normal is a desire for a life in which the things that are special about you are undetectable.

The bottom line is that people aren't interested in being normal and fitting in. What they want is connection. Fitting in is about shaping yourself to meet the expectations of others.

Connection is about finding that which is important to you as well as to the other person.

Connection is sharing the experience of those authentic parts of you together, as opposed to hiding them away and defending against detection.

To fit in, to be normal, takes a significant amount of effort and requires us to deny our individuality in attempting to reach the goal of remaining undetected. It's like walking around all day in shoes that are two sizes too small and pretending they're the most comfortable shoes you've ever had. All the while, hoping no one spots how miserable you are. That level of self-consciousness and sacrifice is no life for anyone to aspire to.

Normal isn't anything that will be of benefit to the individual or society. Sure, we have agreements as to preferred conduct for keeping each other safe and supported as we walk through our lives together.

The one place where it is most essential for each of us to shine and be supported in celebrating our quirks and eccentricities is in our individual relationships.

The friends I have don't like me because I'm normal. They like me because of the benefit having me in their lives brings them. A unique benefit, not a normal one. They are my friends for the same reasons.

My wife loves me because she and I connect in a way we haven't discovered with others. We don't love each other because we work so hard to fit in.

In the end, none of us wants a normal life. What we want is a fulfilling one. A life in which we feel valued, supported, respected and that our life has meaning. Being normal and undetectable will never give you that. All it will give you is the quiet desperation that begs for a life more fulfilling.

Do you Realize that You're Already Living Your Life's Purpose?

"You can't have a plan for your day, 'til you have a plan for your life."—Tony Robbins

Do you have any immediate reactions to this quote? This is something I work on with clients who I haven't seen it worded so simply until now.

What it speaks to is something that eludes so many people and that is: a purpose for their life.

One of the reasons I suspect a life purpose eludes so many is because they think it needs to be something grand, something that attracts the attention of the masses like a Mother Teresa.

In my experience, the purpose of one's life is quite simple. It is to make the conscious decision and effort every single day to share one's gifts with the world.

That's it! Give what you have to give, in order to make your mark on the day in a way only you can.

What I have discovered is that the greatest gift we all possess is our time and undivided attention. No one else can give either of those for you and no one else can give them except you.

The best part of this principle is when you encounter others doing the same thing. You will naturally end up taking care of each other by looking for ways to contribute to the lives of those around you.

How do you find these people?

Live your life's purpose, give of your gifts each day, and those living a similar life will notice you, acknowledge you, be grateful for you, and seek you out.

That is, of course, unless you spot them first.

A conversation of One

"If we all worked on the assumption that what is accepted as true is really true, there would be little hope of advance."—Orville Wright

Have you ever discovered after the fact that someone had made a decision for you and defended it by saying, "I assumed you'd be okay with it?" Me, too.

The reason this happens is because of what I refer to as the conversation of one. Meaning: a person, in her own mind, plays out the conversation she believes she'd have with the other person, complete with the other person's answers and makes a decision based on that conversation.

Here's an example: Let's say she wants to invite a friend to a movie and, without even asking the friend, she has this conversation, "Why don't I ask Cheryl? Well, on second thought, she's been busy lately and she's probably tired so she'd likely say 'No.' I'll just ask Jill instead." Make sense?

Later she finds out Cheryl was not only available but would have loved to see the movie with her.

This is an all too common habit practiced by men and women alike and is a significant saboteur of healthy communication in any relationship.

Why, then, when these assumptions so often lead to hurt feelings do people continue to do this? I'd love to hear your thoughts on it.

Here's a primary reason I've found that explains this. People enjoy predictability and base their "conversations of one" on how their friends have responded to similar situations in the past. The problem with this is that people can and often do change their minds.

The reality is that the past doesn't equal the present or the future. We make our decisions in the present based on those circumstances. The principle I employ to avoid "conversations of one" in my own mind is this: though s/he has responded in one way in the past, I'm going to ask to see if that still holds true for him/her. Make sense?

Always ask to see if s/he still feels that way. I understand, however, and have experienced those who get upset when I ask because their feelings, in fact, haven't changed. They offer responses such as, "How do you think I'm going to answer?" To which I reply: "I respect you too much to assume I know what you're thinking or to deny you the right to change your mind."

You May Keep Your Gift

"You will not be punished for your anger; you will be punished by your anger."—Buddha

Many have told me that I have the patience of a saint. I'll let you in on a secret: it isn't patience. It is simply one of the most profound strategies for setting boundaries that I've ever learned.

I learned this strategy in one of my favorite stories about the Buddha. It was said that the Buddha was a man possessed by an unshakable serenity. He was filled with peace, joy, and compassion that radiated from him.

There was another man, one filled with anger, resentment and hurt. He heard of the Buddha and believed he could find the chink in the Buddha's so called unshakable serenity and so he sought the Buddha out.

When the man found the Buddha, he proceeded to mock him, curse him and throw every insult imaginable in an effort to break him. Alas, the Buddha smiled and was truly unshakable.

The man continued berating the Buddha until the Buddha gently raised his hand and inquired of the man, "Excuse me, sir, may I ask you a question?"

"What?" The man replied angrily.

"If one man offers a friend a gift, and the friend declines to accept it, to who then does the gift belong?" the Buddha asked.

"Well, I guess it belongs to the man who offered it," the man replied.

The Buddha continued, "Well, then, if I decline to accept the gift of your abuse, does it not then belong to you?"

The man fell silent.

Thank You for showing me Who You Are

"I have no room in my life for any form of negativity or non-acceptance."—Ricky Williams

Those who know me know that one of my favorite strategies is gratitude.

Today I shared with someone how powerful gratitude can be at diffusing your anger when someone insults you.

In this case, a young man reported becoming very upset when a friend insulted a sport he really enjoyed participating in.

His initial response is a common one: he felt anger, hurt and somewhat offended. But instead of lashing out he decided to suck it up.

Though he didn't start an argument, he also didn't resolve the anger effectively, so I offered him the following approach for doing so.

One of my main rules in communication is to clarify the other person's intention whenever I feel upset about something s/he said or did. More often than not I misunderstood something and the clarification gives the person a chance to rephrase and better explain their position. This strategy saves everyone a lot of frustration and hurt feelings.

However, what if you clarify and the person responds with the same criticism, insult or negative judgment? That's when I pull out the big guns for transforming anger into gratitude.

I simply say to myself, "Thank you for showing me who you are."

As we search for those who will bring value to our lives we must do a lot of sorting. We are grateful when we find the wonderful people, but often go off on a rant when we find those who are clearly toxic to us.

Wouldn't it make more sense, and be a more pleasant experience to thank them for disqualifying themselves?

Those who make their negativity more obvious are doing us a favor by cutting to the chase instead of leading us on.

So to those who have chosen to criticize, condemn, and complain, "Thank you for showing me who you are." That way I can walk away sooner than later.

When Life goes Other Than Planned

"Life is what happens while you are busy making other plans."
—John Lennon

We all have plans.

We all make plans.

Only to have our plans go, well, other than planned.

What do you do then?

What many people do is pretend that this is the first time it's ever happened. No matter how many times in life we have the experience of planning one thing and experiencing another, many still act as though it absolutely shouldn't happen that way and is a horrible injustice when it does.

It is a horrible injustice indeed. One committed by us toward life.

You see, one of our greatest strengths is resilience. The ability to catch or hit the curveballs of life, instead of simply being hit by them then declaring an injustice.

Every time life goes different, we are handed a sacred opportunity to be resourceful and keep moving forward anyway.

When we do, we also have the opportunity and obligation to give credit where it's due.

The credit is expressed in the form of gratitude for the people and the resources that prepared us for that moment and gave us what we needed to persevere and get through it.

Either that or we can throw a temper tantrum because things didn't go our way. Yeah, why would we want to pass up a perfect opportunity to be dramatic instead of grateful.

The Joy of Disagreeing

"If you have learned how to disagree without being disagreeable, then you have discovered the secret of getting along—whether it be business, family relations, or life itself."—Bernard Meltzer

"We never fight. It's so wonderful." Have you ever heard that claim made by someone?

When you explore that claim what is eventually uncovered isn't a couple in perfect harmony, but a silent decision to avoid conflict. This is a cause for concern.

I've met couples who have spent so many years biting their tongue that they no longer know how to talk to each other, simply because they prioritized maintaining the peace of the moment over the long-term health of the relationship.

I'm not saying it's healthy or productive to have screaming matches over who's right and who's wrong.

I'm talking about two people experiencing a difference in perception that requires them to explore their differences in a respectful way.

Disagreements are one of the best opportunities to learn from each other.

When I give presentations, I invite the participants to challenge and disagree with my ideas. I haven't had every experience there is in life and there is more wisdom in the world than I could possibly learn in ten lifetimes.

So how can I possibly learn more if I walk into any situation with the belief that I have more to teach than I have to learn? The reverse will always be true.

Parents, teachers, and professionals alike, often frame disagreement as defiance or insubordination, and punish it.

This sends the message that having and expressing your own thoughts on the matter is disrespectful whereas compliance is rewarded. Honesty then, becomes a bad thing.

My kids are better at calling me out on my inconsistencies than anyone. I could, though, take the cowardly approach and defend my actions with the all-purpose escape clause, "Do as I say, not as I do."

When you learn to have open discussions of disagreements in a respectful way, it opens the door to increasing levels of honesty because you also learn that your relationship can both handle it and thrive from it.

I'll admit that I'm not always as receptive to disagreements as I'd like to be, but I'm working on it.

Even when I'm not ready to hear it, I still prefer it and the opportunity it gives me to avoid complacency or the tendency to believe my own bullshit. Far too often people hide behind the decree "I have a right to my own opinion" which, of course, is true. More often, though, it is used to put up a mental road block against any challenge of unexamined and highly emotionally charged beliefs.

Friends, couples, or members of any partnership who have silently agreed not to argue or disagree are setting themselves up for lives of quiet desperation.

Lives in which you cannot ask for what you want if it may upset the other person.

A relationship that cannot be fed by moments of honest disagreements and opportunities for growth cannot meet the needs of those involved.

We need to surround ourselves not with those who will argue with and insult our point of view, but with those who will encourage us to reflect upon it.

They encourage it by offering their own point of view. Kindly and compassionately by exploring different ways of looking at life in a way that we both tilt our prisms ever so slightly and now get to see life in a new way.

Life never gets boring when you're able to do that. Life, instead, remains a fascinating journey.

What Pajamas Teach Us about Life

"When you read my books or listen to my podcasts, you have no idea what I'm wearing. I'm a professional because I am paid for the value I provide."—Brian R. King

One morning, my 7-year-old son, Connor, declared a pajama day. He was only wearing the bottom of his pajamas at the time.

So I asked him, "Does that mean if we decide to go somewhere today you don't want to come with?"

He left the room and returned moments later wearing the top of his pajamas as well and asked, "Okay, where are we going?"

Connor is the same boy who a few years ago requested to wear his Superman outfit (cape and all) for a trip to a restaurant. He was well-received and on our way out a fellow patron remarked, "Your kid made my day."

Connor's decision that a pajama day meant pajamas, whether we left the house or not, got me thinking.

Why NOT wear pajamas outdoors, they are comfortable after all.

Lately I've been questioning the role of what one wears and its measure of someone's professionalism. I belong to a networking group for professional speakers and have been routinely lauded for the quality of my message but equally criticized for my choice in wardrobe.

The people-pleaser in me took this feedback very seriously and I went so far as to spend hundreds of dollars on what I was "supposed to wear." What ended up happening is that whenever I presented in what I was "supposed to wear" I felt itchy, hot, claustrophobic, and my already fragile focus suffered, and so did my message.

One day, while watching one of my role models Gary Vaynerchuk present, it hit me. You see, Gary often presents wearing jeans, a wrinkled dress shirt or sweatshirt. That, in addition to cussing like a longshoreman, when he presents.

Gary isn't a role model to me for how he presents or dresses; he's a role model because he is first and foremost himself. No bells and whistles, no pretense, just 100% authenticity and unbridled passion for his message.

Gary is an unfiltered human being in a world of increasingly narrowing lenses. It is in this way that Gary is a tremendous role model for me as I seek even greater levels of authenticity in all that I do.

One of the most beautiful things about Connor is that, at only seven years old, he seems to know who he is. There have been adults, including a few teachers, who have tried to educate his uniqueness out of him, but he has remained true to himself.

So with Gary V's example, my son Connor's inspiration and my wife Cathy's support, I made an executive decision. I would dress comfortably when presenting.

What does that mean? I wear a polo shirt, sport coat, jeans, and sneakers.

Do you know what my audiences tell me after my presentations?

They tell me how much they loved my presentation, how many notes they took and how grateful they were for the strategies I shared.

I have yet to hear, "I had trouble hearing you because of your jeans."

Gandhi wore a loincloth and changed the course of a nation.

I doubt Martin Luther's King's "I Have A Dream Speech" would have lost its luster if he showed up in jeans instead of a suit.

I'm not suggesting that appearances never matter. The reality is that, in many cases, they do and cannot be completely disregarded.

I'm simply pointing out how often we mistakenly believe that they always matter.

When we believe they always matter we can end up putting so much energy into keeping up appearances that once others get the opportunity to get below the surface, there's little substance.

One of my greatest heroes from history is Socrates who was widely reported to be so ugly that he was hard to look at.

He was also legendary for his character and his ability to help anyone he encountered to refine their own.

My heroes aren't the best dressed, they're the best at being themselves, at being human at living their message.

I Have a Story to Tell You . . .

"Miracles happen every day, change your perception of what a miracle is and you'll see them all around you."—Jon Bon Jovi

I had an interesting conversation with my son Zach (age 14) one day and for some reason I explained something to him in a way I hadn't explained it before.

Have you ever had those moments where the right words just seem to come? It's wonderful, isn't it?

Zach was talking about all the difficulties he's had in life and how his "past" has affected him.

To which I replied, "Zach, it isn't your past that has shaped you, it's your story."

Virginia Satir was quoted as saying, "There's no such thing as a meaningful experience, we create meaning."

What I went on to explain to Zach was that your past only refers to the events of your life. But your story refers to the meaning you assigned to those events. Your story, whenever you tell it, is simply a retelling of your decisions about what those events meant to you.

In fact, if you think about it, you'll realize that over the years you've reflected upon many events in your life more positively than when they first happened, right?

Why is that? It isn't because the events changed. It's because your story changed.

As we learn, grow, and reflect, we hopefully gain a different perspective on things we once saw as trials and they gradually become triumphs.

Things we first believed happened to us over time become things that happened for us.

What allows us to reflect upon our more challenging times and create a new story for our lives? It's an amazing quality called resilience.

It's our ability through a form of mental alchemy to turn any event in our lives into something we can use.

A story of doors opened and opportunities created is yours for the telling.

I'd love to hear your story.

Just Keep Swinging

"Great works are performed not by strength but by perseverance."—*Samuel Johnson*

My son Connor (age 7) is very energetic and is always in motion.

Waiting for the bus to arrive each morning isn't something he's prepared to do. He wants to be active.

So, many mornings Connor will say, "I want to hit the ball." There was plenty of time this morning so I gladly offered to pitch to him.

Now we're talking about someone who couldn't throw straight if his life depended on it. I'm not known for my coordination by any means, so I would just have to do my best.

Connor swung at every pitch I threw whether it was waaaay over his head or well off to the side. He even managed to hit a few and give me a little exercise as I chased the ball down.

But what made this moment special wasn't how many hits he made. It was his seemingly endless enthusiasm for swinging the bat.

He didn't seem concerned about missing the ball, he simply took a shot. As many as it took to hit the ball.

How many of us hesitate because we're afraid we'll miss? Connor has realized at a very young age that you have to keep swinging.

My role was just as important. Every time he swung the bat I never made reference to the fact that he missed. All I would say is, "Alright, let's do it again."

My focus was on how important it was to keep going. Didn't hit the ball? Okay, keep swinging.

Sure there's success to celebrate in getting the hit. But you're not going to experience it if you don't first make the decision to keep swinging.

17 Ways to Respect Feelings

"You cannot make yourself feel something you do not feel, but you can make yourself do right in spite of your feelings."
—*Pearl S. Buck*

1. You can never say the wrong thing while listening.

2. Understanding what a person said isn't the same as understanding what a person meant.

3. If you become upset by something a person said, ALWAYS clarify—perhaps you misunderstood or she chose her words poorly.

4. If you only think of things in terms of right or wrong, you have a 50% chance of getting upset each time you interact with someone.

5. If a person insults you, he is speaking from his own pain. It isn't about you, so you can let him keep his pain and go on with your day.

6. When someone asks for your honest opinion, ask her if she sincerely wants it and give her the opportunity to withdraw her request.

7. Only give advice you're qualified to give. Don't guess at a solution simply because you want to be helpful.

8. Don't ask someone about a problem you aren't willing to help him solve.

9. Don't say anything about another person you aren't willing to say to her face.

10. Gossip is not a life skill.

11. A sincere compliment can brighten the darkest day for anyone.

12. Speak in terms of what is working and what will work even better.

13. Realize it is rare to hear someone right the first time; always clarify.

14. The more you say, "can't", the fewer options you have.

15. Saying "No" more often and at the right times allows you to keep your focus on the things that really matter.

16. Whenever possible, before you speak, ask yourself this question. "Is what I'm about to say going to improve my relationship with this person?"

17. What you say to others will be only as kind as what you say to yourself.

How to Be at Your Best

"With realization of one's own potential and self-confidence in one's ability, one can build a better world."—Dalai Lama

Have you ever gone to the zoo? Fascinating place, isn't it?

Even more fascinating is how the creatures inside the cages seem to be more civilized than the ones outside.

I accompanied my son, Aidan (then nine years old) on a class field trip to Brookfield Zoo. I went primarily to have a day where I could give him my undivided attention, and in part to protect him.

Aidan has Autism and is fragile in so many ways. I feared the parent chaperone he was assigned to wouldn't know how to support him with so many other kids in her keep, and I feared how he'd manage the other kids and the chaotic environment of the zoo.

Little did I know that the experience I was in for was the opportunity to watch my little guy shine. He did not need my protection, but he did earn the deep admiration of those he was with.

There were three things that made that day work really well:

- SPF 100 sunblock

- A quart of Gatorade

- And my undivided attention

Whereas the other kids in the group seemed to be more interested in going to the gift shop, getting snacks, and spending the money they'd brought with them, Aidan and I were more focused on being together. As we planned for this day, in fact, the focus of our conversation was about just being together.

We were going to be at the zoo together, we were going to spend the day together, we were going to enjoy being together. The details of what we ended up seeing were secondary. It wasn't about seeing as many animals as we possibly could, it wasn't about making sure we walked out with a dozen souvenirs—it was just about having that time together.

Another important thing that made this day really special is the fact that I had absolutely committed to "being there" and only there. I wouldn't think about what I needed to do the rest of the day when the field trip was over. I wouldn't think about what I'd be doing if I stayed home instead of taking the day off.

I was committed to making sure that my attention was fully on being with him because there was absolutely nothing more important during that time.

I want to ask you a question and I urge you to answer it honestly. How often does your child want your attention, but you ask your child to wait while you attend to something trivial like a television show? When you do that, each time you do that, you are telling your child that in that moment, television is more important than he is.

I admit that I often get caught up in my own projects. I get hyper-focused. I just want to get it done and I, too, have made the foolish choice of making something more important than attending to one of my children.

So I was determined to make sure that for this day that it would absolutely not happen. I had nothing else planned. I had nowhere else to be but right there with my son.

I don't remember the last time I'd ever seen Aidan so happy, so excited, and so engaged with what he was experiencing. Perhaps I hadn't ever been as engaged as I was at the moment. One of the coolest things about Aidan is his gift for seeing incredible amounts of detail wherever he goes.

I've seen this when he draws. I've seen this when we take walks and he's able to pick out the smallest flower—a flower, which seemed to be hidden from view from everyone but him. He is particularly gifted at reminding me to stop and simply be aware.

I was amazed when I saw this gift for spotting detail come to life at the zoo, and how it enriched the experience of the entire group. It occurred when we entered the reptile house.

Prior to that, we were outdoors; the animals were larger and easy for everyone to see. But in the reptile house it was dark, it was cramped and most of the cages were small, with smaller creatures.

I repeatedly heard others saying, "Where is it? I can't see anything, it must be hiding." Aidan was able to look in any cage and within seconds spot where the animal was, even if it was camouflaged and only a small part of its body exposed. He wasn't even wearing his glasses.

At school, Aidan is shy, afraid to speak up, socially excluded and often bullied because of his differences. I often worry about him because of how others respond to the way he stands out.

But today he stood out alright—he was at his best. I saw others looking to him to show them where to look and what to look for. I saw him taking the lead and contributing to the group in a way only he could. That is what it means to stand out.

As we left the reptile house to enjoy the rest of our day together, I observed the stark contrast between how Aidan conducted himself and how the other boys in our group behaved.

One boy in particular never seemed to be satisfied. He was frequently turning to his mother and demanding she buy something for him, as though he expected to receive it. When she said no he would whine incessantly, ignoring her efforts to redirect him.

At one particular point, I asked his mother for permission to ask him a question, she agreed. I asked him, "When you woke up this morning and began getting ready for the day, were you happy?" He looked at me blankly and his mother said, "I remember, you were happy."

I then asked, "Did you have the toy then?" Again he stared blankly. I concluded with, "If you were happy this morning without the toy, is it possible you could still be happy without it?" He dropped the subject.

Aidan didn't ask me to buy him anything: why? Because our being together was our purpose, our having experiences (not things) was our purpose.

Later, I heard this other boy again asking his mother to buy something for him, an item far more expensive than his first request. When she told him no, he made a statement that stopped me in my tracks. He said, "Maybe Aidan's dad can help pay for it."

I turned to him and asked, "Do I have a say in what I spend my money on?" He dropped the subject. Toward the end of the day, as we were walking toward the exit, I felt someone step on the back of my shoe. I turned around and it was this boy, with a smirk on his face.

I was grateful to this young man and his mother. I was grateful to see what a marvelous young man I have the privilege of calling my son. I was grateful that when Aidan and I interacted with each other we did so with mutual respect and gratitude.

I was also grateful that Aidan is the one I got to take home.

Later that day I reflected upon how those few hours with Aidan became so fulfilling. Let's look at the word "fulfilling", it means to be fully filled with your experience.

When I planned to spend that time with Aidan, I chose that nothing would enter that space with us. It was just him and me. I cleared my schedule; I had no emails to check, no calls to return, and only one appointment to keep. I had an appointment to be with him and only him.

My commitment to give myself fully to that time allowed me to be fully filled with that experience, and Aidan's cup ran over as well. I received one hug after another throughout the day, and dozens of smiles.

At the end of the day, when I had to see him off to his bus back to school, he said, "One more thing." Then he gave me the biggest hug I ever remember him giving me as he said, "You're the greatest dad in the whole wide world." I hugged him, told him I loved him and that he was my favorite Aidan in the whole wide world.

Those moments we spent were so abundant and so wonderful that I asked myself why on earth I don't have them more often.

Do you ever have moments so full? Do you experience them often enough?

The reason we don't have more fulfilling moments is quite simple. It's because we allow those moments to be filled with other things, thoughts about the past, worries about the future, thoughts of judgment and frustration.

How often do you attend to such thinking that doesn't allow you to be at your best?

Aidan and I were fully at our best in our time together. I am at my best when I am writing this for you, telling you of this experience that taught me so much and hoping it will benefit you as well. I am at my best right now because I'm giving this my full attention instead of rushing through it.

I encourage you to look at the areas of your life that you prioritize. Do you give your time, energy, and attention to a job you know takes more from you than it ever gives you in terms of opportunities to be your best, because you aren't allowed to use your gifts fully?

Are you involved in relationships in which you feel held back because your best results in jealously from others?

Do you deny yourself your best because those you've chosen to be in relationships with will be left behind if you step into your potential?

Do you fear that by being at your best you risk being alone because so many don't believe enough in you or in themselves to step up with you?

I speak from experience when I say I understand the fear of changing jobs when you have a family to support and don't know whether the decision is the best one.

I know the pain of ending friendships, the devastation of divorce, even when it was a relationship that left me feeling unappreciated and undervalued.

I also know the experience of working through these changes and coming out the other side. So I can also tell you how magnificent life can be when you move beyond those experiences that prevent you from being your best. Then committing yourself fully to the efforts and relationships that bring out the best in you.

It's hard work to believe in yourself sometimes. It's risky to go after what you truly want for your life.

When you don't let up and you finally get it, it's the most wonderful place to be. But you won't create it while giving your time and energy to the things that don't bring out the best in you.

What brings out the best in you?

Why You Should Always be Perfect

"The thing that is really hard, and really amazing, is giving up on being perfect and beginning the work of becoming yourself."— Anna Quindlen

"Nobody's perfect." We tell each other that all the time in a well-meaning, hypocritical fashion. Hypocritical, when you don't allow yourself the same courtesy.

Why do you work so hard to achieve perfection while comfortably letting others off the hook?

Here's a thought: you lack so much confidence that only in a state of perfection can you avoid any and all criticism. Thoughts?

You see, perfection, as people tend to define it, is the only state in which there are no mistakes and therefore nothing to criticize. No openings for someone to question your performance, your judgment, your intentions, etc. That is, no openings for anyone except you. We both know that while others are applauding your efforts, a part of you is waiting for one of them to detect the screw-up and criticize you. WOW, what a way to live.

I'm not saying it's wrong to want to be perfect—there are plenty of benefits to perfection.

Let's consider a few:

You aren't allowed to be less than perfect. Let's face it, once you've achieved it, why would you settle for less? You're a role model now; others look up to you to see how it's done. You don't want to let them down, do you?

You get to do everything right the first time. How awesome would that be? No more trial and learning, no journey to your goal, no adventure. You get to bypass all that excitement, the buildup toward that sense of victory. Who needs it anyway, right?

You get to know everything. Imagine what it would be like to not have to learn anything new. When you're perfect, you know everything—how it's done, everything you need at the outset. You're like Nostradamus on steroids. How great would it be to lose your sense of wonder just so you could avoid the possibility of criticism? Wouldn't it be great?

With all that said, yeah, being criticized can hurt. But going through life feeling like you're never good enough, because you still have something to learn, hurts more. So here's what I'm going to do:

I'm comfortable being a role model. In fact, I can say with utmost confidence that I model imperfection, humanity, vulnerability, ignorance, and teachability extremely well. I'm a 100% homegrown human being and damn proud of it.

I want the adventure of life. If we never have the experience of climbing the mountain, we can never appreciate the view from the top, let alone show anyone else the way.

I don't want to know everything. If I did, I wouldn't need anyone else. They'd all be coming to me for the answers, and then who would I have to look to? That would be awfully lonely.

Now that I think about it, imperfection has a lot more to offer. Yeah, I'll go with that.

After all, nobody's perfect. Wait, something about that idea doesn't work. Who wants to be a member of the Nobody's? I don't.

I want to be a part of a "We."

Instead of saying, "Nobody's perfect."

Let's start reminding each other that, "We are all still learning. This lesson is for you. Go with it and grow from it."

Thanks for the Humility

"Humility is the only true wisdom by which we prepare our minds for all the possible changes of life."—George Arliss

Just when things start going really well, life often has this sadistic way of throwing something in your way, doesn't it? Okay, less sadistic and more opportune. After all, without a little resistance, it's difficult to build muscle.

In my case, life threw me gout—look it up and read the description of how painful it is to get a little context. It happened a few years ago, right before I had to go out of town for a speaking engagement.

As an introvert, one thing that had always made navigating airports more bearable was that I could be quiet, not have to talk to anyone (except TSA) and otherwise disappear in the crowd. Not this time.

Having great difficulty walking, I struggled with how on earth I was going to get from home, to the airport, to the plane, etc., with a painful, swollen right foot.

Well, I drove to the airport, quite gingerly putting pressure on the gas pedal instead of living out the NASCAR fantasy I typically do when in a hurry.

Upon arriving at the airport I found the only parking spaces available were four rows from the back of the lot. I'd borrowed my Mom's cane (thanks, Mom) but what did I do?

I left it in the car. Why? Because I had brought two carry-on bags instead of a roller bag, because I hadn't accounted for how much difficulty I'd have in balance with a cane.

I made my way to the tram that took me to the terminal. Here's where my comfort zone got thrown right out the window. I had to check in at the customer service desk to request the wheelchair service. I'd reserved it the night before with the encouragement of both my mother and my wife, Cathy.

A very pleasant woman with a foreign accent helped me into the chair and through security. All the while saying, "Excuse me" so that people would turn around and look at us before apologizing and stepping aside. She even cracked a few jokes that were difficult to understand, but she tried. She offered to stop by the restroom or at one of the restaurants if I wanted to get something to eat.

She was so kind, but I had no idea how to allow myself to be helped in this way. I can be so self-determined at times (Don't say "typical male" here!) that I don't contemplate doing things otherwise. This is known as taking things for granted.

So this pleasant woman left me at the gate to wait for my flight after making sure I had everything I needed. I waited for the boarding to begin and enjoyed about an hour of fading into the background.

As the boarding began my name was announced over the loud speaker to give me the opportunity to board sooner in case I needed help. Awkward! But again, the gentleman who called my name was very kind.

When I arrived in St Louis and made my way off the plane, just outside the door was a gentleman standing behind a wheelchair with a small sign that said "B. King." Another very kind gentleman stopped "us" by the restroom, so I could take a personal break before transporting me to the gate where the hotel shuttle would bring me to the hotel.

Let me say that the cramped seat and air pressure change does not improve foot pain and swelling.

So there I was, in my hotel room reflecting on the day thus far and what I was able to take away from all I had experienced that day. What I took away from all this was the lesson pointed out to me by my dear wife Cathy a few nights earlier.

I asked, "Why, when things start to go so well, does something always seem to go wrong with my body?"

She responded, "Maybe to teach you a little humility." She was and is right. I'm learning that it is important at every step of this journey that I remember the important lesson that I preach most, the importance of interdependence. Of helping and being helped, of partnering with others in order to meet our needs.

As much as I prefer the background in public places and avoid social interaction as much as possible, I am finding that the more life provides me with opportunities to teach; it also provides me with opportunities to learn.

Such is life, so ends the lesson (for now). Lesson learned.

How to Stop Wasting Your Time

"You know, you only get to live life once, so there are two things that that yields. One is that there's no point in crying over spilt milk, but secondly you hate wasting time, energy, and whatever talent you've got."—David Miliband

I've had many conversations about how people choose to waste the one thing that is the most valuable and irreplaceable source of abundance in their lives... their time.

I want to strongly encourage you to take a serious inventory of how you spend your time and what you've got to show for it. Make a list and seriously look at it through the lens of, "How is my life better as a result of spending my time in this way?"

Let me share some of the discoveries I've made.

I stopped watching TV about two years ago, I thought, because I'd gotten too busy to fit it in. Then one night my wife had a reality show on and I was intrigued enough to watch it with her. The next thing I knew I was talking to the TV and being upset at the stupidity of the people on the show.

I literally turned to my wife and said, "Did I just talk to the TV? What the heck is that about?" She said, "I know, I think it's funny, I've never seen you do that before."

It then occurred to me that this is why I stopped watching TV. It is a source of frustration and I don't want to spend my time feeling that way. From the evening (bad) newscasts, to over-dramatized television shows that run me through a roller coaster ride of emotions. I felt like I spent a few hours having my mind jerked around, accomplished nothing during that time and wasted time I'd never get back.

You may argue that there are educational programs, too, and those other programs are there to give yourself a break from life for a while.

I agree there is an abundance of amazing educational programming these days. My personal standard is that it's only educational if it provides knowledge I can use for more than water cooler conversation. If it doesn't improve my life, or help me improve the lives of my children or my clients, I don't see how it's a good use of my time.

In addition, if you need TV to distract you from your life, then you need to change your life instead of changing the channel.

But why do that when you can do what's easy?

I've met countless people who live their lives according to the Martyr's Creed of: "I'm only happy when I'm helping others." What makes this approach martyrdom is when you don't require reciprocity; you give as though you have a bottomless well of time and energy that doesn't need to be replenished.

You don't take care of yourself and feel guilty at the suggestion of doing so. So I ask you, how is your life improved by spending your time in this way? You spend your time; sad, exhausted, feeling like you can never do enough because you haven't made everybody happy yet (including yourself). In the end, you'll have a long line of people waiting to eulogize your selflessness while you're continuing to fret over all of things you have yet to do.

The bottom line here is that we are here as human beings not human doings.

How much time do we spend in line, in traffic, and otherwise waiting, to get to the things we want to spend our time doing?

Until you value your time enough to no longer tolerate others wasting it or taking it for granted, you won't set the boundaries that make the difference between a day that energizes you and leaves you feeling better and a day that leaves you feeling exhausted and no further ahead than when you started.

A colleague and I were discussing how often we hear how we're unaffordable, when in reality, we ask for far less than the value we provide.

What we realized is that our culture conditions people to feel entitled to more, for less. Cheaper is seen as preferable to the overall benefit. She put it best when she said, "Some people will choose to spend five years with a therapist who will save them money instead of investing in one of us and seeing faster, more meaningful progress in a shorter amount of time."

Here's the most powerful observation that she added, "They don't realize that they can always make more money but they'll never get that time back."

By investing in yourself and making better use of your time now, you improve the quality of your life, sooner than later. This goes for anything you procrastinate, spending time sitting on your butt instead of exercising, surfing the internet mindlessly instead of starting the book you've always wanted to write.

Why do you make money more important than your time?

Why do you prioritize being busy, over simply being?

I'll leave you with this. How are you spending your time today?

Why are you spending it that way?

What do you want to change and need to change to feel that this day was time well spent and something worthy of celebrating instead of bitching about?

When will you take the time to change it? No one controls your schedule but you.

Only you can waste your time.

The Meaning of Life is Next to the Snow blower

"The best way to find yourself is to lose yourself in the service of others."—Mahatma Gandhi

A few years ago, during a particularly harsh winter, I had a conversation with a young man who I'll call Dan. He was looking for direction in life and knew he wanted to be of service somehow. I asked him to think about what being of service meant to him. He didn't know.

I defined service for him this way: service is giving of yourself, time, efforts, or resources, to solve a problem for someone else. With that, I asked him if he'd been of service to anyone in the past week. The example he offered really touched my heart.

He received a call from a friend of his father's, who we'll call Bob. Bob offered him $25 dollars to clear the snow from his driveway. Dan jumped at the chance to make a little extra money and accepted. At some point, he reflected upon Bob's current situation.

He knew Bob was on a fixed income and had amassed a sizable debt because of recent health problems. So when the job was done and Bob offered Dan payment, Dan said, "Why don't you keep the $25? Merry Christmas." Needless to say Bob was extremely grateful.

Dan could have easily said, "Hey, I wish the guy well, but he promised me $25 so I'm going to collect." Instead, he demonstrated selflessness, integrity, and compassion.

Most of all, he was living from the very place of service he aspired to be, without realizing it. Dan had been thinking of service as something found in a career after college graduation. He didn't realize service is more of an approach to life.

As Dan and I reflected upon this experience, I helped him see that the service he provided Bob went beyond giving of his time and effort. You see, service doesn't lie solely in what you do, it is also provided by the spirit in which you do it.

He gave of his generosity in a way that created an experience for Bob. An experience in which Bob felt compassion being extended to him; he likely felt cared for during very tough times.

Dan helped create a meaningful experience for Bob. Dan took the time to care about Bob, to be of service to Bob as a person. When someone is impacted personally by what you do, your act of service takes on greater meaning.

We also discussed those simple acts of courtesy many of us are taught, practice sporadically, and often give little thought to beyond. The "I do it because I'm supposed to, or because it's how I was raised."

Something as simple as opening a door for someone can remind him that he matters.

I shared with Dan one of those meaningful moments that made such an impact on me that I still remember it. A few years ago, I was walking into an office building and saw a gentleman maybe 50 feet behind me approaching the building.

I could have easily gone into the building and taken care of my business. But this time I decided to wait. When he approached the door, I opened it for him. He smiled, and what he said next is what has stuck with me to this day. He said, "Thanks for noticing me." He didn't say the customary, "Thanks." He said, "Thanks for noticing me."

That's when I learned why we do these things for each other. It isn't just to be polite; it's to take the time to notice each other. To take a moment to show another person that they are significant and for that moment you are demonstrating that they're significant enough to you that you paused to offer a simple gesture of kindness.

Life has far more meaning when we consciously extend ourselves, our time, our efforts, and our resources in the spirit of noticing one another, and giving each other those moments of significance. If we could do this more with each other, I suspect we'd feel like we meant more to this world. Then each of our lives would have a lot more meaning.

Connection through Social Media

"If opportunity doesn't knock, build a door."—Milton Berle

What is the last door you walked through?

Why'd you walk through it? Because what is on the other side is preferable to where you're currently standing, right?

The people in your life are there for one main reason; they realize there is a benefit to knowing you. Talking to you brings value to their life. Engagement with you gives them more value than not talking to you, right?

What if you lived with the awareness that every engagement with another human being was an opportunity to provide value? The first question I ask myself each morning is "How can I add value today?"

The rapidly growing world of social media has provided us a platform to impact people's lives for the better, like nothing that has come before.

Even if you aren't a fan of Facebook, and the rapidly growing influence of social media, you'll still find value in this section because the bottom line is, it's still about relationships.

If you don't yet follow me on Facebook, I hope you decide to, because you'll be able to see everything I discuss here in action.

Let's talk about Facebook in the context of business, since that's what I primarily use it for. Specifically, I use it for the purpose of relationship marketing. What does that mean? In my mind, relationship marketing begins with the relationship, not the product or service.

This approach is very different than traditional marketing, which consists of finding ways to interrupt you with billboards or commercials. Relationship marketing is about building rapport, establishing trust. It takes a little bit longer, but, guess what? You'll get loyalty like you wouldn't believe.

You're not looking for a quick sell. You want to establish brand loyalty by creating a personal connection with the people you serve.

You need to build the relationship first. You have to actually know and care about the people you're serving. The old days of crunching numbers to measure the number of widgets sold per quarter to nameless, faceless consumers has been reinvented on social media.

Sure, you have to work a lot harder now, but, wow, is it ever more meaningful and fulfilling when you actually know the faces and concerns of the people you're helping.

Remember this always: being connected on social media isn't about how slick your website is or how awesome your product is. The thing people are connecting to is YOU.

Why you? What makes you so special? Why would they want to connect with you? Why should they care? Why should anybody friend you on Facebook, connect to you on LinkedIn or follow you on Twitter? Why?

Is it simply because they like you or is there more to it? Is there something more substantial that they need to have with you?

Yes: trust. How is trust established?

By consistently providing something of value on a regular basis, you earn their trust. Consistency and reliability are the foundation of trust.

The people you trust are the ones that you know, and know how they're going to show up. You don't have to wonder if the person that you saw last time is going to be the same person this time, right?

Consistency, reliability, and trustworthiness are characteristics you must have when you show up anywhere in your life. Whether it's with your clients, your family, on Facebook or whatever—when you post something, they know it's you. When you tweet something, they know it's you. That consistency, that trust, and that value is the reason people choose to connect with you and stay connected to you.

Well, how do you know what's going to be valuable to them?

Ask. The best thing about social media is that you don't need to hire a marketing firm, you don't need to cold call, or do a lot of heavy research, you just watch and listen, see what they care about, see what their problems are, and if it just so happens that you can provide a solution to that problem, do it.

We are there to provide solutions, to provide opportunities to walk through doors. That's what we do. Are you posting links to articles? Are you sharing inspirational quotes, pleasantries?

What options are you providing them, that they can come to see you as the primary source for?

You want to show them the opportunity door, and most importantly, you want to demonstrate to them consistently that you have all the faith in the world in their ability to walk through it.

It's not simply, "Here's a quote, go be inspired." People will respond to that quote, they'll respond to that article. Some of them will respond with gratitude. Some of them will respond with doubts, with cynicism. And you will be there through the art of the conversation to support them and potentially shift their perspective on what their options are.

What I post comes from a desire for discussion. Every comment on every post is an opportunity for you to respond with value. You could invite them to consider something else. Don't tell them; don't preach; don't lecture. Simply offer.

You are there to show them the door, not pound into their head how they absolutely must walk through. That's lecturing. Relationships are not about monologue. They're about conversations. It's critical that you use social media in the same way.

One of the most amazing things about social media is people often forget that others are lurking, quietly observing what they're putting out there day after day. They'll put something out there about the difficulty they're having with their child or at work.

All of a sudden you post something that's uniquely relevant to their situation that provides them just the insight they needed and they say, "Oh, it's like you read my mind." No, I read your status update.

But don't tag them in the post. You simply put it out there for them to find or message it to them privately. I am blessed in that many people have told me they look at my profile first thing in the morning to see what I've posted. Knowing this keeps me on my game so I make stopping by worth their while. They have gotten used to looking to me for consistent value.

Unfortunately, there will always be what are referred to as trolls. People so invested in their own negativity that they would hijack an otherwise positive post and inject their own pessimistic worldview. They will often stoop to name-calling and personal attacks in order to keep the attention on themselves.

It is up to you to set the tone on your profile. What is the standard of discourse? When you post complaints, you're inviting misery. "Hey, I'm miserable. Who wants to join me? I'd like some company in this."

Set those boundaries quickly and consistently so people realize you have a higher standard of discourse on your profile. If they don't like it, they're welcome to leave.

One way to view people who post on your profile is as a guest in your house; they are there with your permission. You don't show up to their house with all your negativity, all your judgment, and all your criticisms. Why would you do that to somebody you care about?

It's important to simply remove these people from your network if they won't remove themselves. You are not obligated to help everybody. Your mission is to support those who are supportable.

There are some people who will argue for a massive list. That's not my philosophy. I want quality, I want engagement.

The following I have didn't happen overnight. It took several years. Social media is like any other relationship it takes time. Time for them to watch you and get to know you.

I make a point of using it deliberately to provide value, not to provide the latest "whine and complain" that I have in my day. Sure, there are far too many whose updates read like a roller coaster ride of drama and mediocrity, and all points in between. They're not using it strategically like I do.

People have said to me, "Oh, I'm not really into Facebook. I really don't like Facebook." "I'm not into all the whining and the drama."

My response to them is "Fine, don't do that, then." Social media is what you make of it. If you don't whine and complain you will not attract those people. You won't find whiners and complaining in my network because they can't stand my frequent posts about confidence-building and personal responsibility.

An important part of what you share with your network is your story. That's where your value comes from. Your life is the main source of your inspiration, your power, and your message.

When you talk about your life, you're telling your story, who you are, where you were, where you are now, and how you got here.

As you observe the statuses of those who follow you in social media, you're learning their story and whether or not they like their own story.

What's on their minds? Are they looking forward to something or dreading something?

So, if you want to provide value, you want to be somebody who's there to provide a new door to walk through, how do you know what door to provide them? Look at what door they're looking at now. Read their updates.

You don't need to respond with your ten-step program solution, that if they enroll today their life will be wonderful. That's not what you're offering them. You're offering them the opportunity to consider just one door other than the one they're currently looking at.

How many steps does it take to walk through a door? One... two tops, right? So when you're offering them a suggestion, and you're inviting them to consider something new, it only needs to be one step further than the step they're currently on.

I see many people post things that are grand epiphanies and people dismiss them as pie in the sky because they're so far off from where they're at now.

You can't empower anybody to consider something they do not believe is possible for them. So you always want to give them something that's just one more step. One little shift—that's it.

Now let me give you some ideas on how to do all of this strategically. Remember, nothing goes on my profile by accident. Everything has a purpose. One thing I do every now and then, because the people who follow my profile closely realize I'm not a complainer. I'm not a critic. I'm not a whiner. I celebrate the possibilities. But every now and then, I will put a "frustration" up there.

On one occasion, I posted how my middle son Aidan decided he wanted to play with matches. That was a big issue in our house. I handled the problem when it arose, and didn't feel like a victim.

I posted it to create a "Me too" opportunity for the people in my network, so they could share their experience and create a discussion around it. They then get to experience a feeling of contribution and of being supported.

My post simply stated, "My kid was playing with matches and I'm not happy." Whoosh! What resulted was one of my longest conversation threads, simply because it was such a shared experience.

Once again a part of my story was similar to a part of theirs.

Ultimately, what are we trying to give people an opportunity to do in their lives? Help them make a buying decision?

Decide whether to hire us or not? What are we helping them do? We're helping them celebrate their own story and consider a different story if they choose.

Your entire brand, believe it or not, is not about a product or service. Your brand is you. Your story is what people are buying into. And the more your story intersects with their story, the more they will know, like, and trust you, because you're just like them. But more importantly, you're a little bit further along the journey than they are—which is why they need you, because you can show them how to go those extra steps.

You know what doors to walk through. You know why to walk through them and what's on the other side, and you can teach them how to do it. The way you demonstrate this to them is not through a sales pitch; it's through conversation.

One thing that irks me a little bit is when I see other professionals post, "Are you having (such and such) problem? I can help. Link."

My approach is to prove I'm helpful by actually being helpful! Show them an article that provides them that one step further. Give them a word of advice that provides them one more step, one little tweak in their thinking. You're being helpful.

You're being helpful in the very specific areas that you get paid to help people. It's amazing how many people will message me and say, "You're really good at this relationship stuff. Do you do this?" "Well, as a matter of fact, I do. What questions do you have? Or have you checked on my website?" "You have a website?"

This is what happens when you show up each and every day sharing insights into how they can rewrite their story. You're not telling them what to do or that they should do it. You're simply recalling a time when it's something you decided to do and the results you experienced when you did. Make sense?

When they're ready to see how your story is eerily applicable to their life, they'll thank you for sharing your story with them.

Each day is like a new episode in an ongoing drama. There are cast members, story lines, etc.

I talk about the story of my business, my marriage, and parenting.

As you watch others tell their story, they'll tell you all about the results they want, the actions they took, and the results they actually got.

They'll share what their beliefs are, what options they feel they have, and what they think they're personally capable of accomplishing or changing about their circumstances.

Then, every time you post something, every time you put something out there, you're giving them a door to walk through.

An essential part of your story are the doors you've discovered, how you arrived at the decision to walk through each of them, and what you experienced on the other side once you entered a new room of possibilities.

As you work to build the relationship with the people in your network, you are using your own story to help them get in touch with the limitations in their own stories.

You show them how your story isn't so different from theirs, to read about where you've been and say, "Me too."

Then show them the door(s) that let them know where you were to where you are now. If they decide to walk through, they create the opportunity to share the "me too" of now with you, as well.

Hey, I've been there. I hear you. I know what you're talking about. I had the same problem with my kid when my kid was your kid's age. Would you like to know what I did about that?

That last question is critical in building relationships in social media. You must get permission to advise, especially if you've reached out to them personally. Okay?

When I was first becoming acquainted with social media, I learned through experience and a lot of backlash, that just like in offline relationships, there are times a person simply wants to be listened to and not advised.

So simply ask the question. Which would you like from me? Are you simply posting because you want to vent or do you want guidance?

"Oh, I have some ideas on that. Would you like to hear them?" Sometimes they'll respond, "Sure, message me." They'll want it privately or they'll say, "Sure, what have you got?" and you can share it on their post.

Under those circumstances, you hopefully give them exactly what they need and their connections will be a witness to what you have to share as well.

Permission is a key component to relationship marketing, because people want to feel supported by you, they want to feel cared for by you. They don't want to feel like you're in their face, with old style heavy marketing, "buy, buy, buy, now's the time, limited time only, limited supplies".... People hate that stuff.

You know what they want more than anything? People who care—so care! The value you provide, first and foremost, is caring attention. The value you provide is the fact that you "get" their story, because you, at one point, shared that story with them and now, when they realize that, hey, somebody gets it, the person who gets it (you) is not as stuck as I am.

What I'm sharing about relationship marketing is simply how I've learned to do it, what works for me. If what you're doing is getting the results you're looking for, you're doing it correctly, for you and your tribe.

So one of the most important questions to ask yourself is: what is your story? What is their story? What are you prepared to help them do, to change their story, and how do you let them know that you can do that?

One of my favorite quotes is from Kevin Welch. It reads, "There will be two dates on your tombstone and all your friends will read them but all that's going to matter is that little dash between them." The dash is your story.

What do you stand for; what do they stand for? Where are you going and where are they going? How are you going to somehow meet them somewhere along your mutually shared paths and take the journey together?

There are too many people out there who have a story of problems. That's when your story of problems, which pave the way to solutions, can be helpful.

They make one decision and you propose another.

The new door that you have to offer is a brand new story with brand new opportunities.

So, before going out there and actively engaging in social media, the first question you need to answer for yourself is what's your story? "What's your story?" in terms of where you were, where you are now and how you got there. Every client, every person you're ever going to work with, comes to you for one reason, because you have a door and they don't.

It's not as simple as, "What's your problem? Okay, here's your solution." You're not teaching tactics, you're teaching philosophy, you're teaching beliefs; you're helping them polish their lens or giving them an entirely new one. That's what a relationship is about.

You're building likeability, you're building trust, and you're building a connection. You're not just priming the pump of prospects to sell them stuff. That's the difference between just simple sales marketing and relationship marketing.

Are there specific steps for successful relationship marketing? I'd say the first is perseverance, don't give up on it. It's an experiment, an adventure.

The second one is listen. People will tell you what they want and need, if what you're doing is aligned with them, then let them know it, with their permission, of course.

Remember that anyone who wants to offer you a blueprint for relationship marketing can only tell you what worked for them. They can't guarantee you it's going to work for you. You're not them. You don't have their story.

No matter what the steps are, you have got to effectively be able to communicate your story to them, that you care, that who you are is authentic, genuine, and more importantly, able to help them to see themselves in your story.

You must be able to show them how your stories intersect.

You are where you are now. I was there, too, in some ways. I'm at this place now. Would you like to be here now, too, or in some form? So what conversation do we need to have? How do we need to rewrite your story so that you can see yourself following a similar path?

It's not simply, do this and you'll get results, do that and you'll make a million dollars. You need to think, feel, and act differently. If you have one story, you think, feel, and act one way. If you have a different story, you think, feel, and act an entirely different way. It's all about the story.

Staying engaged in their story is a way of becoming part of it. You can like it, comment on it, or share it, to show that you are paying attention.

One technique I've noticed that works consistently is that people will check my profile after I've liked something on theirs. This is a great way to invite the very person you want to help to stumble upon your latest post.

Pay attention to them, show up, and acknowledge what they care about too. Then you'll remain in their awareness. You don't have to come up with something clever or say something profound all the time. Just be there. Just care. Just let them know you're paying attention.

One of the things I've gotten into is the habit of wishing everyone on my list a happy birthday. Facebook has a feature that reminds you of when everyone's birthday is.

Even if it's somebody who connected with me a year ago and I don't even remember their name, they're in my list so they thought enough to friend me at some point, right? So I make a point of sending a happy birthday greeting. It's wonderful when people respond as though you made their day, even though the two of you don't correspond, because you still took the time.

One of the other things that's important for me is to say something different on each person's page. Have a great day, happy birthday, happy happy birthday.... You want to be unique, stand out. You want top-of-mind awareness. I put things such as: "Have a super fantabulous birthday! I hope today is absolutely magnificent. I hope today is filled with as many smiles for you that you give everybody else."

Don't just sit there with a list and say, I'm going to cut and paste today. Let it come from the heart. Be authentic because you want to build trust with them. Under no circumstances should you be a phony to save yourself some time.

It's a lot of extra work to build relationships, but that's why it's worth it. You're here to do something purposeful; to do something that matters, and the best way to do that is to impact people where they live. They live in their life. They live in the moments. They live in their story, so take your story, merge it with their story, and before you know it they have new experiences that they never even considered was possible for them—all because you showed up.

Does This Life Make my Butt Look Big?

"Failure is simply the opportunity to begin again, this time more intelligently."—Henry Ford

Like a pair of pants, you won't know if a new experience or opportunity is going to be a good fit for you until you try it on.

Have you ever been presented with any opportunity only to feel some resistance toward it? Saying things to yourself like, "Why do I have to be here?" "What if I don't like this?"

Questions like that set you up to anticipate pain. Where's your curiosity? Why not approach it with a sense of wonder instead of impending doom?

Be an experiential detective who is looking to see what's there. Look to collect evidence through experience and then decide.

New experiences give us the amazing gift of showing us one more example of what life has to offer. My oldest son Zach is an extremely picky eater and only eats about 5 or 6 different foods.

He's so comfortable with limited options that he's decided any new foods, which aren't one of the current 5 or 6, will suck.

Unfortunately, he tends to extend this scarcity thinking to relationships as well. He recently finished his freshman year of high school and expressed concern about going back because he "didn't like the other kids." Upon further examination, he approached meeting people the same way he approached food.

Meet as few as possible then make grand generalizations about everybody else.

Would you try on one pair of pants, then declare, "These don't fit, I can't wear pants" then give up on pants, even though there are many racks and sizes to go? Of course you wouldn't, that's absurd.

A simple fact of life is that you simply won't know whether you like it or not until you try it on and that includes experiences. A few years ago I decided to take a ride in a glider, even though I have significant motion sensitivity.

I was practicing what I preach here. I wanted to know what my actual experience of flying in a glider would be instead of assuming it would be dreadful. There were some cool things about it, such as how quiet it was, but whenever it turned or changed altitude it felt like putting my intestines through a blender.

But now I know. I know it, instead of simply assuming it. In our 400-channel world, not every moment of life needs to be entertaining to have value. Experience doesn't waste our time;

we waste our own time when we fail to do the work to find value in it.

Time is always well spent when you walk away with knowledge. Even if that knowledge is as simple as "now I know". I promise you that of all the experiences you have in life; the vast majority of them will be try-ons.

That's the only way to get to the ones that really get inside you, help you discover who you are, and light you up. This is fun, this is boring, I like this, I don't like that, I feel happy when I do this, I feel sad when I do that.

Only through having experiences can you sort all of that out. Avoiding new experiences creates a situation where you have trouble finding out who you are and what you need. Life is to be experienced, so try it on as often as you can.

And don't stop until you discover the one that's a perfect fit for you.

The Joys of Quitting

"Learned helplessness is the giving-up reaction, the quitting response that follows from the belief that whatever you do doesn't matter."—Arnold Schwarzenegger

Sometimes I look at all that I've accomplished in my life and all that I plan on accomplishing. My greatest leaps forward began when I quit doing something that was keeping me stuck and started doing the thing that would move me forward.

I have written numerous lists over the years to help keep me on track. One of the most powerful lists, however, hasn't been written until recently. It's the list of things I have quit doing and must remember to quit doing so that I no longer stand in my own way.

This list of my greatest quits and quits to come is by no means comprehensive. It's a start and I'm planning to spend more time on it in order to unlock even more of my potential. I hope this list resonates with you and compels you to become a bigger quitter for your own good. You deserve it.

1. I quit listening to my inner critic and start listening to my inner coach. The coach that tells me that I am made of more and deserve to become it. This isn't about being perfect; it's about working to be aligned with the contribution I want to make to this world.

2. I quit blaming other people for how I feel about myself and for how my life turned out. Then I started listening to the people who build me up instead of tearing me down. My own family members played a significant role in the devastatingly low self-concept that plagued me for much of my life. Then I realized the world was filled with people who had more to offer me in the ways of building myself up and started listening to them.

3. I quit believing life isn't fair and resigning myself to the short end of the stick. Those who get repeatedly screwed in life are the ones who continue trying to play by a set of rules that don't work. So I started changing the rules or creating new ones. Society tells us you need a college degree to succeed, and yet there are hundreds of success stories in which people left the classrooms that weren't teaching them what they wanted, so they found mentors to guide them and now make millions of dollars a year, improve the lives of countless people, and do it with an education that wasn't acquired in a traditional way.

I'm not knocking education; I have a Master's Degree. I have acquired a far greater education since graduation and much of it has come from unlearning the limited thinking of my degree.

If I'd believed that, I would be destined to spend my life in a social work practice, working 15-hour days, never seeing my family nor having a life. I wouldn't currently be working from home, setting my own hours, spending more time with my family and working with clients all over the world, as I am now.

The shift occurred when I stopped believing the lie of "the real world." Watching what everyone else does that makes them miserable while saying, that's the real world. Listening to people who insist I must be someone I'm not in order to succeed in the real world. What a load of horse poop.

The real world (are you paying attention?) only refers to things I cannot change. It doesn't refer to the things I refuse to do the work on *to* change.

4. I quit believing there are things I CAN'T DO and started asking for help to learn how to do them. When I suggest this to people they offer absurd examples like, well, men CAN'T have babies. Comments like that are a feeble attempt to distract you from the fact that people don't walk around holding themselves back in life because men CAN'T have babies and people CAN'T flap their arms and fly.

We hold ourselves back repeatedly by telling ourselves that we CAN'T do the things we sincerely want for ourselves, when the reality is that we refuse to ask for the help we need in getting them. I CAN'T is often code for I WON'T. It's hard to do it so I WON'T do it. Changing this pattern, for me, began with the humility I found in the statements, "I don't know." and "Will you help me please?"

5. I quit complaining about not having friends and started learning how to be a friend. When you expect everyone else to change, as though you play no part in the solution, then alone is how you'll remain. I was sick of being treated like crap by so many people and being rejected by the opposite sex. So I set out to discover the tools that would help me be more effective. Pay attention when I tell you this: NONE of them required me to change who I am. What they do is allow me to be more effective in communicating who I am.

6. I quit saying I can't afford it when it comes to the things that will improve my life. I started asking, "What do I need to do to be able to afford it?" and I was amazed at how resourceful I became. People will live in misery and settle for less when it comes to getting the guidance they need. But they'll make sure they pay the bill for their 300 cable channels every month so they can chat about what's happening on their favorite show. That is, when they aren't spending time bitching about the things in their life they refuse to put the necessary effort into changing. I experience the change because I prioritize it and do the work. It isn't because I'm special or smarter, have more luck, or more resources.

7. I quit trying to be right about everything and started working to be more effective. This requires that I change my focus from my ego to the results I'm getting. I constantly examine and question the results I get so I can

improve upon them. Those more interested in their ego, and wanting to be right, spend more energy making excuses and defending the crappy results they end up experiencing over and over.

8. I quit blaming my disabilities for the problems of my life and started asking the question, "How do I succeed anyway?" What I discovered was the power of partnership that allowed me to accomplish the things I want in nonconventional ways, as well as the "allowing of myself" to utilize the positive aspects of my learning differences.

9. I quit living in a past that I wish hadn't happened and started doing whatever it takes in the present so I do not repeat it. This began by realizing that all of the bullying and other horrible things people subjected me to over the years weren't about me and therefore weren't a statement of my self-worth. People who feel bad do bad things. Yes, they did hurtful things to me but I'll be damned if I inherit their hurt. They can keep it while I grow stronger.

10. I quit avoiding responsibility then started using these phrases more often, "How can I help?" "Will you teach me how to do that?" No longer avoiding present opportunities that help me build my future.

11. I quit trying to make everyone else happy and started focusing on the happiness found in the relationships with those people who truly appreciate what I have to offer and are eager to return the favor. Life can be exhausting and

miserable when we believe that we're in the convincing business. That we somehow need to convince people that we're worth their time and that we're good enough etc. Quit wasting your time on those people and that way of thinking.

So what is the overall message here? It's simple. Your life is yours, to create and to advocate for, without waiting for someone else to do it for you.

You must speak up in every way you can, with your voice, with your writing, and with your actions. The only way your needs can ever be known is when you let others know what they are. The only way others can meet your needs is when you tell them how they MUST be met.

You are the leader of your life—take charge.
Don't expect others to simply know the way—show them.
Stop waiting for life to come to you—create it.

Love

Your First Thought of The Day

"The greatest weapon against stress is our ability to choose one thought over another."—William James

You've heard it a million times: "Practice Makes Perfect", right? The question is, what are you practicing?

In one of my favorite movies, *The Peaceful Warrior*, there is an exchange between the two main characters, Dan (a college-aged aspiring gymnast) and his soon-to-be mentor, Socrates (as Dan would later nickname him).

Dan has put all of his time and focus into mastering gymnastics in order to qualify for the Olympics. This "all-eggs-in-one-basket" approach has led to atrophy in the other areas of his life. Outside gymnastics, Dan thinks little of himself, has poor relationships, and frankly doesn't know what the hell he's doing.

So as Socrates observes the sloppy life Dan has created for himself, Socrates shares this observation with Dan, "Dan, you know the difference between you and me? You practice gymnastics, I practice everything."

What did Soc mean by that statement? He meant that while Dan gave his undivided attention to the mastery of gymnastics, he (Soc) gave his undivided attention to mastering his life.

I work with many people from all walks of life and, without exception; they come to me in a similar state. They have focused so hard and so long on mastering thoughts and behaviors they *don't* want...procrastination, negative thinking etc.

The reality is that they're very good at these things because that's what they've been practicing all this time. If procrastination gets your focus and your effort, you're going to get damn good it, and a lot of people are.

The key to changing this pattern is found in a question posed to me by one of my mentors. He asked, "If your life were the most important thing in the world to you, how would you treat it?"

Far too many people treat an aspect of their life (career, family, a single relationship) as the most important thing and guess what happens? The other essential aspects of life wither out of neglect because they starve from lack of attention.

When contemplating what it is I do professionally and personally, I've wondered why I believe I'm on this planet. This is what I came up with: I'm here to connect—to connect with this moment, with others, with my passion and to hopefully help others do the same.

Having struggled with connection my entire life, I decided at age 35 (now 43) to immerse myself in the study of how we connect so I could master it and make it the one thing I excelled at instead of it being my greatest weakness.

I succeeded. Why? Because I gave it my undivided attention.

What was my greatest discovery about connection? That it is the meaning of life. The more deeply we connect with ourselves, with others, with nature, and with our purpose, the more fulfilled we are, the more we live and the more we give to this world.

So my question to you is, how's your practice coming along?

What was your first thought today? Don't know!

What was the first thought you remember having today?

Consider that moment when you decide the kind of day you're going to have. You and I both know that decision affects the way you relate to the people you encounter throughout the day.

How many people do you know who dread Mondays and make it known to the world? Are you one of them? There is only one reason Mondays suck and that is because the first thing Monday morning people wake up and think, "Ugh, Monday. Now I have to go to work when I want to sleep in." That opening thought to your day sets the tone for your experience of that day.

What's even worse is how many people conspire together to make sure that Monday sucks so they can connect with each other around that experience. "Mondays suck, don't they, Tom?" "Yeah, Bill, they really do. I think they should be outlawed."

Now Tom and Bill feel like they've connected with each other because they shared an experience. Do you see the problem here? If they start the day feeling connected over their conclusion that Mondays suck, their Monday then has to suck so they can stay connected. Heaven forbid Bill should suddenly have an experience that makes Monday go great.

What would happen if he told Tom how great his Monday went? Tom might be jealous and resentful, so Bill either doesn't tell him or he pretends his Monday sucks.

Have you ever done that? Felt guilty about feeling good because it might threaten your connection with someone else?

I see this with far too many support groups, not all, but many. People come together to discuss their difficulties and what eventually happens is the Tom and Bill scenario. Once you establish connection over something negative, you may feel obligated to maintain that point of view and that experience to remain connected.

If you then decide to be positive, to grow a little and improve your circumstances, you risk criticism from the other group members who accuse you of oversimplifying things, having rose-colored glasses or whatever it takes to encourage you to doubt yourself, so you fall back in line to the negativity that brought you all together.

It's amazing how many people will sacrifice happiness and growth in their lives in exchange for feeling connected.

Do you stay in relationships that hold you back because you feel your only alternative is being alone?

So many of my clients share stories of quietly enduring relationships with relatives that beat them down and leave them feeling drained because they've been taught to respect their elders, which requires them to accept such treatment.

No offense to anyone's upbringing, but I see no value in expecting the next generation to indulge your masochism.

Our primary obligation to those who follow in our footsteps is to lay a path worth following, not leave them saying, "I hope I don't end up like you."

My wife, Cathy, and I walked through an oriental-style garden one day, and while enjoying its long-weaving trail, I noticed a sign that read, "Stay On The Path." I turned to her and said, "Consider the implications of that sign."

That's what I encourage you to do. Consider the implications of the path you're on as a person, a parent, and a colleague.

What your life has been is now and where it is going will remain the same as long as you remain in relationships that obligate you to remain stuck in order to connect with people.

I have a recommendation for you. One that is surprisingly simple and can radically improve the quality of your day.

For the next 7 days I encourage you to begin each day by sharing your first thought of the day with someone else. The first thought that you decide will be the defining thought for your day.

Then at the end of the day you are to share with that person what actions you took to make sure that the day went as planned.

Now I'm not talking about the "Mondays-suck" thoughts. I'm talking about taking charge of the thinking you do to prepare you for your day.

This will require you to be more aware, more responsible, and more deliberate about the thoughts you decide to grab hold of in the morning.

Thoughts such as:

"I'm going to be grateful today. I'll do that by thanking everyone who helps me and let them know how much they matter to me."

"I'll be accepting today. If something doesn't go as planned, I'll remind myself that I'll be okay, I've done it before and I'll do it again."

"I'll acknowledge my self-worth today. If someone treats me well, I'll acknowledge that I'm worth it. If someone treats me poorly, I'll acknowledge that I'm still a worthwhile person."

Are you in? Awesome!

You Have to Compromise, Right?

"A compromise is an agreement whereby both parties get what neither of them wanted."—Author Unknown

"Sometimes in relationships you just have to compromise." You've heard that one before, right? I had that conversation with a few parents recently and a pattern emerged.

They were describing frustration, and at times exhaustion, as they recounted outings with their children that were intended to be enjoyable.

As we dug deeper we discovered something I also experience. Often parents and their children have different temperaments. I move more slowly and want to take the world in gradually; my two younger boys tend to be full steam ahead. The other parents I talked to had a similar experience.

As a result their outings with their children felt like a tug of war of needs with one or both parties feeling as though the other were standing in their way of having a good time.

Then, at the height of frustration, a parent would announce, "Look, we have to compromise here." A discussion would follow about how "you can't have everything you want and you need to agree to give up a few things".

Does this conversation sound familiar? What tends to happen is that both parent and child walk away feeling as though they had a "less than" experience because they had to compromise.

May I offer an alternative to compromise that can make all the difference?

Compromise tends to have a focus on scarcity. Meaning that, "we both can't have, so one, or both, need to give up something." The moment you have that conversation, it's important to realize that what needs to be a shared experience has become competing experiences.

Is this why you're spending time together? Nooooooo. You're spending time together because you want a shared experience—a shared experience with a child who lives at a different speed than you do most of the time.

So how do you meet in the middle so you can get your needs and your speeds to match a bit better? By asking this important question of each other as you plan your time together. Ready? "How do we take care of each other during our time together?"

This question shifts the focus back to where it needs to be: on each other. Our time together isn't about the activity that we happen to be doing together. It's all about us. We come first, the experience is second. If we both aren't enjoying it, sharing it, then why are we doing it?

When we attend to each other as part of what makes our time together successful, it is difficult to get caught up in "the me, me, me" that can make compromise necessary.

What tends to happen, then, is a shift to "the we" which is the focus that we wanted in the first place.

What's Good about This?

"The pessimist sees difficulty in every opportunity. The optimist sees the opportunity in every difficulty."—Winston Churchill

It's the little things in life that matter; did you ever hear that one?

This saying is the absolute truth and, believe it or not, is the secret to happiness. Now hear me out before you shout "baloney" or some other colorful term in response to this assertion.

Regardless of whether things are going the way you want in life or not, the reasons are the same. You are consistently making the decisions and applying the strategies to create those results, right?

When you want to change the results you're getting, all that's required it a little shift. It starts by making the decision that a shift is needed

Here is the moment of truth where 98% of people blow the opportunity to make the shift. In that moment of insight, when it occurs to you that, "You know what, the way I've always been doing this doesn't work for me. In fact, it tends to make things worse. Let's do something different and see what happens."

Then, after that moment of clarity, you say, "No, that's not it," or "That'll never work" and then go back to the same old garbage you were doing.

You have an opportunity so many times a day to shift what you're doing and you don't do it because you're married to your current way of doing things.

The fact is, the shift can only begin when you have these moments of clarity (which happen more often than you realize) and listen to them.

Resourcefulness, as you know, refers to your ability to find solutions in a situation instead of getting obsessed with the problem.

The key to being resourceful is a simple but powerful question you must ask yourself whenever you experience a challenging situation. That question is, "What's good about this?"

As someone who has survived cancer and a horrible divorce, this question is even more valuable because the first answer to that question can be, "I get to learn how to move forward from this better and stronger." Solution-focused thinking is critical in situations like those.

Of course what we're talking about here is making little shifts in everyday life as well. By getting into the habit of asking this question, you'll soon discover that nothing can slow you down or hold you back.

In relationships particularly, misunderstandings are perfect opportunities to ask, "What's good about this?" Each one teaches you where communication can break down, or where it already has broken down, so you're always refining your communication skills.

When generating solutions, it's important to realize that there are no perfect solutions; there are only the best solutions you create in that moment.

You apply them, get feedback, refine them and apply them again until you find the one that ultimately works best.

One of the biggest saboteurs of the solution-generating process is the "yes but."

It prevents you from seeing what's good about a situation because you end up disqualifying it with the fact that there's something that isn't good enough about the situation.

For example, "Thank you for cleaning the mess up but you shouldn't have made it in the first place." See what I mean?

Here's how you can effectively remove the "yes but" permanently from your thinking. Ready?

Whenever you catch yourself in a "yes but," immediately cut off the second part of the statement and say it again.

For example, "Let's do (a particular thing) to solve this problem, but what if it doesn't work?"

This statement will now become "Let's do (a particular thing) to solve this problem." Then you apply it, get feedback, refine it and apply it again.

I'm sure you agree that life is filled with less than perfect situations, right?

Do you also agree that in those situations there is still plenty to be happy about?

Of course, as soon as you remove the "yes but" you see so much more of what the situation has to offer, just a little shift.

Because as long as your focus is on the "not good enough", you will always be upset with the situation, but when you focus on the part of it that you can be grateful for, suddenly everything is so much better.

That's one of the many things that's good about this.

Time and Attention

"Until you value yourself, you won't value your time. Until you value your time, you will not do anything with it." —M. Scott Peck

When it comes to relationships, what matters most to you? What do you remember? Do you remember the content of the conversation necessarily, or do you remember that moment of connection—the moment when you felt understood because someone else truly listened to you and "got" you. Does that matter more to you?

That's what relating is. It isn't about shooting the breeze, killing time, or making chitchat. It's about connecting with another human being.

It's about realizing and honoring the fact that the person across from you had a choice to be anywhere else and they chose to be here, now, with you. You have chosen to give me your attention by reading this book.

In return, I want to hold the space we've created together and honor the fact that I have that attention, and I want to give you that same quality of attention back.

When you're relating to someone else, please start from that point of reference. You have both chosen to be here and time is the one thing we will never, ever get more of. We have this moment together and that's it. Do you agree?

This is one thing you have in common with everybody else you'll ever meet, whether a stranger, a colleague or your life partner, you have this moment in common. What do we do with it?

In some respects, it depends what that person means to you.

Is it someone you're intimate with, or are they a bit further removed, such as a friend, colleague, acquaintance or stranger?

Do they all matter regardless of how close they are to you?

Yes, absolutely. And what's really fascinating is how fluid their position in your life can be. Each person in our lives was unknown to us at some point. People who were once strangers become acquaintances and soon friends.

My best friend from childhood was my right-hand man for twelve years. But upon graduation from high school we drifted apart and I can honestly say we have very little in common these days.

People move in and out of your life quite regularly. The absence of those closest to us is, of course, the most noticeable.

What do you believe determines the role that people play in your life? How close can you and they eventually become?

Is it the amount of time you spend together?

Can you spend a lot of time together only to discover that you still have very little in common? Of course you can. Time gives us more opportunity to connect, but doesn't increase a likelihood that commonality will suddenly develop.

What ultimately determines who you permit to become close to you, versus who remains a stranger, boils down to your criteria for who gets to play a given role in your life. Who gets to be close to me? Who do I let in? Who gets to see my vulnerability?

Let's think of this within the context of creating moments together. Let's say that you're in one emotional state and you want to move into another state, from sad to happy for instance. Is there a person in your life you can count on to cheer you up?

The person you place in that role is someone you allow yourself to be vulnerable with. Someone you allow in when you're feeling sadness. Someone you trust to join you in that moment and help lead you to a state of happiness.

Now remember, this person's responsibility is not to make you happy. This is someone you trust to create this experience with you. That's the key. You have chosen to allow this person to create that experience with you.

In business, acquaintances are very helpful. In this age of social media I have a vast network of acquaintances I regularly reach out to when someone closer to me needs information. It is wonderful how often my acquaintances respond by being helpful. I'm eager to reciprocate whenever possible.

Before the World Wide Web, we were limited to those with whom we had regular face-to-face contact. But now, the world is our community and geographic proximity is no longer a prerequisite to connection.

The beauty of having so many acquaintances is that each of them brings unique gifts to this world. Gifts that may not fill an immediate need of yours but may do so for other people in your network. The greatest use of your network is as a community where people can come to help and be helped.

There are people who judge the quality of their life by the quantity of people in it. This is a trend on social media as well. You and I know that a pound of gold is worth more than a pile of gravel. It's about accumulating value, not volume. Every person in your network should be there because you are providing reciprocal value to each other. Think long and hard about that.

Social media creates a unique opportunity to create intimacy with people you'll never meet. This book can have the same affect. Though people who follow me online, or you and I for that matter, may never meet, this exchange of information between us is a way of relating to each other.

One important question I ask myself before writing these words for you, speaking to others face to face, or sharing something on social media is, "Where's the value?

I've got their attention. Now, how am I going to use it?

How am I going to value their time? By realizing that what I put out there is going to move them somehow. Am I going to whine, complain, criticize?

Relating is about showing up in that moment.

When you show up to whine you are inviting people to share that experience with you. Is that truly the experience you want to create with them? Would an experience of creating a solution be more useful for both of you? Then ask for that.

There is essentially one common experience we all want to have as human beings.

To believe and feel that we matter is an experience we're all hungry for. It is an experience you can create for a friend or a stranger.

How do you do it?

By expressing gratitude for the time and attention they're giving you in that moment.

What they're doing for you is giving you their attention. When are they doing it? Right now.

Imagine how much more you'll appreciate the value of others when you show up and live from that mindset.

So who are your intimates? Who are your friends? Who are your acquaintances? Why are they there? Are there some people that you want to move around? Are there some people who are intimate who really have been messing up the job and they need to be reassigned a new role in your life?

Do you have friends who you want to bring a little closer? The only way you can really move people in either direction is to know what your criteria are.

People are in your life and in your heart by permission, not by entitlement.

Giving someone your time and attention doesn't require a grand gesture. It can be so simple. If you get someone a cup of coffee, it's not because s/he wants coffee, it's because you think enough of that person to take your time to get it and bring it to him or her because s/he matters.

When you do it from that place within yourself, it takes on a whole new meaning. I guarantee it will feel different when you do it in that spirit, than if you're just completing a task.

Please Expect More of Me

"We are a community and we will only reach our greatest potential when each of our members makes their full contribution to helping each of its members grow." —*Brian R. King*

Have you ever uttered the words "Accept me exactly the way I am" or "I'm perfect just the way I am."

Those statements they can be taken to mean at least one of three things:

1. Don't judge me for how I am

2. Don't try and change me

3. Don't ask me to grow

Though I expect these statements are inspired by the first possible meaning, they are most often emphasized by people asking for the last two.

When I married Cathy, I was excited about the adventure I knew we'd take together. I knew I would become better in every way and I hoped to be such that she'd be comfortable doing the same with me as her life partner.

One thing I wanted from Cathy was her acceptance of the person I was, but I also wanted her to help me become more, to grow, and become the best version of myself. Together we're accomplishing that in spades.

Growth as a person and as a couple is simply not possible if I require her to accept me exactly as I am and ask nothing more.

I am NOT perfect just as I am because perfection is not an accomplishment—it is more of a delusion that prevents you from allowing yourself to be challenged to grow.

All of life's challenges can make us or break us and each one of them helps us grow, if we let it.

On one level I don't so much want to be accepted for who I am. I simply want others to get to know who I am so they can make an informed assessment, instead of a rash judgment on little information.

Then I want them to challenge me. Don't allow me to become complacent, lazy and stagnant, or sit still in any way.

Like every living thing, we are given this life to grow and not simply stay as we are.

The acorn needs an opportunity to maximize its potential as an oak tree.

Yes, in the beginning it needs to be acknowledged as an acorn and spared judgment for not yet being an oak tree.

But, at no time, should it be told "Stay exactly as you are, don't change a thing." Instead it MUST be encouraged to "Show me what you've got."

Do you Want Respect with That?

"Respect is what we owe; love, what we give."—Philip James Bailey

In our increasingly automated, drive-through world, the experience of customer service is a dying art.

More often these days we're asked, "Do you want fries with that?" by someone stuck in a scripted hamster wheel hell.

At our local grocery store, we hear the same questions each and every time: "Did you find everything okay?" and "Do you have any coupons?" asked by an often expressionless cashier watching the clock until his/her next scheduled break.

There are exceptions of course, there always are, and it is one of those exceptions that I'd like to share with you.

My wife and I have the option of shopping for groceries at the local megastore that advertises the lowest prices, which, of course, are offered at the expense of customer service, and fellow shoppers who forgot their manners at home.

Then, there's the smaller family-owned grocery store. It's more expensive but the value far exceeds anything listed on the sales flier.

My wife, Cathy, shared a story with me about an act of overwhelming respect, courtesy, and consideration she witnessed while shopping at our local, family-owned grocery store.

It was after a particularly heavy snow and she saw an elderly man leaving the store on a mobility scooter provided by the store for its patrons.

As he was crossing the busy driving lane in front of the store to reach the parking lot, his cart loaded with groceries, stopped as the battery died.

This frail gentleman attempted to stand and retrieve his groceries, which he would then need to lug through the snow to his car.

Just then Cathy watched as the young man who was collecting the shopping carts from the parking lot intercepted the elderly gentleman.

This young man encouraged the gentleman to sit back down on the scooter. Then with all his strength he pushed the man, his groceries and the dead scooter all the way to the man's car.

Once there, he placed the groceries in the man's trunk and assisted the man into his car to make sure he did so safely.

Finally, this young man pushed the scooter back into the store.

Cathy placed her groceries in the car and returned to the store where she hoped to find the young man to express her gratitude for what she'd just witnessed.

She couldn't find him but she did find the scooter, plugged in with a hand-written note explaining that it was charging and encouraging patrons to select another one.

Who says the young generation is lost?

I continue to have experiences in which I hold doors for people only to be greeted with looks of shock and expressions of gratitude when those whom I took the time to notice explain that, "No one does that anymore."

I've noticed, as well, that we don't seem to see each other anymore. What's up with that?

Where has our attention gone, to our cell phones perhaps?

Wherever it's gone the result is that we've forgotten about each other in so many ways.

We act more like we're in each other's way when the reality is we're each other's company as we make our way through this life together.

I hope you'll reflect upon this with me as I offer you a promise.

In this life I am with you. I see you and I respect you.

Will You be The First?

"Honesty is the first chapter in the book of wisdom."—Thomas Jefferson

People can be so competitive, can't they?

Somebody's always shoving to be first in line.

People who want to be right, every single time.

These firsts can be pretty lonely.

Who was the first person you thought of this morning? Was it someone who upsets you, or someone you love?

Your first thought of the day sets the tone of the day. Are you moving forward or holding back?

You see, winning in life isn't about being first overall.

Winning in life begins with the first things you do each day, every day. Not yesterday.

For someone else, today your words could be the first they hear. Will they be caring or critical?

Your smile may be the first another person sees today, and may end up meaning as much to them as the sunrise.

I didn't invent the world, I wasn't the first person to walk upon it, but I can work to make it better.

I wasn't the first in line, but I can be kind to the others who form the line with me.

I wasn't the first to feel love, but I can make sure those who are loved by me know it.

When it comes to doing what it takes to create the life you want, the first step will always be yours.

When NOT to Put the Needs of Others Before Your Own

"You don't get extra credit in this house for being a martyr."
—Cathy King (my wife)

The value which states, "You are supposed to put the needs of others before your own" is one of the most misunderstood values there is and far too often becomes a one way ticket to martyrdom.

Those I've talked to who have the extreme version of this belief decide that it is their obligation in life to be so devoted to others that their needs don't matter. Many live with feelings of guilt and desperation as they silently chastise themselves for being "selfish" when all they're doing is having the momentary realization that they have needs too.

Well, let me set the record straight with my interpretation of the value that: "You are supposed to put the needs of others before your own."

It means that when you are considering an action, that you should consider how it might impact others as well. By thinking of how it might impact others **first,** you decrease the risk of making an impulsive and purely self-serving decision.

That's what this value means. Think of others first as a way to make sure the needs of others are considered in your decisions as well.

It doesn't mean consider them INSTEAD OF yourself or at your expense.

You can't water a garden with an empty pitcher and we aren't placed on this planet to audition for sainthood.

We're human beings and every single one of us has our own needs, many of which we look to our relationships with others to satisfy.

Don't let your epitaph read, "Here lies someone who loved me unconditionally, went above and beyond to make my life wonderful, but refused to allow me to return the favor."

To Find the One, You Must be The One

"Authenticity is the alignment of head, mouth, heart, and feet—thinking, saying, feeling, and doing the same thing—consistently. This builds trust, and followers love leaders they can trust."
—Lance Secretan

Are you searching for "the one?" That perfect person that will give you everything you need in a relationship.

I hear many people talking about wanting to find "the one", whether it is the person they'll be married to for life or the person who will finally accept them for who they are.

One thing I've discovered in life is that you don't find the one by looking for the one. You find the one by being the one. Let me explain.

You get what you are in this life. If you're selfish, you'll be surrounded by people who take advantage of you. If you're helpful, you'll find people wanting to help you. If you are a kind, loving person that's the kind of person you'll attract because people want to be with people who are like themselves.

Here's where this idea breaks down, however: when your kindness is an act, instead of authentic.

When you're pretending to be kind but secretly resent the people you're being kind to then don't be surprised when the people you surround yourself with are also resentful, frustrated people.

You get what you are NOT what you pretend to be. Make sense?

The one (in my experience) is the one who balances you out in your areas of challenge better than anyone else. Of course there's more to it than that, but let's focus on this aspect because it's a critical one.

In order for you to be ready for that person to enter your life, you need to be humble enough to allow that person to be better in your areas of challenge than you are, and you need to be grateful for it.

This requires a level of vulnerability and surrender that is at the heart of the deepest connections between two people.

Agreeing to create this kind of relationship with another person takes a special kind of courage that most people aren't willing to practice.

How do you begin to develop this courage to lay the foundation for such an amazing sense of connection with someone else?

In my experience, it begins with a shared compassion for each other. The realization of a shared compassion that you both have the same basic needs as human beings, the same fears and the same desire to be safe and respected in your most vulnerable moments.

Through your shared compassion, you agree to welcome each other into those areas of vulnerability, to allow their strength to become your strength and vice versa.

Those are the moments when you don't know where you end and the other begins. That's connection.

Why the Shortest Relationships can Mean the Most

"People come into your life for a reason, a season or a lifetime."—Author Unknown

It's amazing how some of the most meaningful relationships in your life can be the shortest.

The reality is that every relationship we have is a short one, because it only happens a moment at a time. Each moment we add something new to it, to help it grow, and it becomes something new. Those short spans of time are the building blocks of our lives.

One of my favorite quotes is, "A person comes into your life for a reason, a season, or a lifetime."

I've counseled many people who fret and fit over the ending of a relationship and say things like, "All those years wasted."

Wasted? Why? Because it ended.

In our ongoing effort to prevent change and hang onto the things we love in life, we often fall victim to the belief that things hold their greatest value when we can keep them.

WRONG!

People, Places, and Things have their greatest value when we appreciate them.

I admit, when my marriage to the mother of my boys ended after 12 years, I had that same reaction, "Well, there goes 12 years down the drain."

Then I realized that's like graduating from high school and saying, "Well, there goes 12 years down the drain." What about the education? What about the memories? Those haven't gone anywhere.

Why do so many come to the end of a chapter in their life and feel time was wasted simply because it ended?

It's because they fail to realize that its value lies in the fact that it's temporary.

The lessons of my failed first marriage have made me a better man, a better father, and (hopefully) an amazing husband to Cathy, my wife, my best friend, and the woman with whom I have the privilege of waking with every morning.

I wake up each morning with gratitude and the realization that every day I need to be someone worth being married to.

That means showering her with moments. Moments in which I remind her that I choose to be with her more than anyone else; moments in which I tell her how grateful I am that she chooses to be here.

I remind her each day of the reasons I choose to be with her. Those moments build upon each other and form the seasons of our lives. Cathy and I just celebrated the end of the 3rd season (year) of our marriage and the beginning of another that we have the privilege of creating together.

What reasons do you have to maintain certain relationships in your life? Do you remind your friend, partner, and colleague of those reasons?

Through these relationships, are you growing or "slowing"?

Reflect upon each relationship from its beginning to the present. What have you learned? What decisions have you made? How are you better now because this person has been part of your journey?

How would this person answer the same questions about you?

There's only one relationship that lasts for a lifetime and that's the one with YOU. You're the only one who gets to experience the journey from start to finish.

We have many reasons and seasons that come in and out of our lives to support us on the miraculous journey called the human experience.

You allow me into your life for a reason and hopefully for a season. For that I am grateful.

Please pay it forward.

A Little Support, Right When You Need It

"I've always thought that people need to feel good about themselves and I see my role as offering support to them, to provide some light along the way."—Leo Buscaglia

When you surround yourself with those who have your back, it's easier to take the bigger risks to grow because you KNOW you aren't going it alone.

Isn't it amazing how much more courageous we become when someone who believes in us is right by our side.

I'm sure you remember the scene in the movie where the fighter pilot has the picture of his best gal tucked into one of the gauges in the cockpit right where he can see it.

You've noticed how your child stands a little taller on stage during the winter concert when he notices you there.

Like two strands of rope or the double helix of our own DNA, we are stronger when we're bound together somehow.

Sometimes we are at our best, are more empowered, and hit the winning home run when those who believe in us are physically present. We feel them watching, we can sense their pride and their love.

You hear the calming voice on the other end of the phone reminding you, "You can do this." Then suddenly the distance between you disappears and you can almost feel their hand resting on your shoulder.

When I travel to present I always open my suitcase to find a note from my wife, Cathy. She's playful and finds new places to hide it. Sometimes it's right on top so it's the first thing I see, or it's slipped into a shirt pocket or slid into a shoe.

Though every note she writes varies in it's wording, the message is always the same. She loves me, she thinks I'm amazing, and knows I'm going to be awesome. Most —she believes in me.

Though she can't always be with me physically, her love is there, her loyalty is there, her confidence is there.

The confidence I feel knowing that she is there in that moment and in my life is a constant reminder that, though I am walking my own path in this life at times, I also have someone walking by my side and sharing the journey, someone who believes in me.

The way that I believe in you.

Family

Being Considerate

"Being considerate of others will take your children further in life than any college degree."—Marian Wright Edelman

One of the greatest things you can do for the people in your life is to refine your character.

Each of us knows someone who seems to only think of him or herself. She seems to make decisions based on the criteria of what will please her right here and right now.

The consequence of this way of thinking is often a ripple of pain emanating outward as others suffer due to her self-centeredness.

I suspect you know what I'm talking about and can remember a time you were on the receiving end of this.

If you're being honest with yourself, you can also remember a time you were on the *causing* end of this. I know I can.

The key to being aware of this tendency, habit, whatever you want to call it, is that when you know better, you can do better.

You can decide at any moment of your life to raise your personal standards so you can raise the quality of the results you experience in your relationships, and therefore in your life.

Here's a suggestion for improving upon the tendency to seek pleasure in the moment without consideration for others.

When you are about to speak a word or take an action, as often as possible, ask yourself this question...

"Will what I'm about to do or say send ripples of pleasure or pain beyond this moment?"

The answer to that question will guide you well.

How am I Doing?

"Criticism, like rain, should be gentle enough to nourish a man's growth without destroying his roots."—Frank A. Clark

How do you define *confidence*?

For the purpose of our conversation, let's define it this way: confidence is the belief in your ability to be effective. People who believe they're going to screw up all the time either don't act or procrastinate.

An important thing to remember here is that being effective doesn't always mean you get the result you want. What is more important is knowing what to do with whatever results you get.

It isn't about creating relationships in which misunderstandings seldom occur, it's about being able to spot them the moment they occur and knowing what to do to resolve them and to keep moving forward. That's the kind of confidence you want to develop.

Easier said than done right? So what do you do if you're lacking confidence? You begin by understanding that the reason you have low self-confidence is because of a critical step in building self-confidence that is missed. A step that people aren't even aware that they are taking.

That single step is the question you subconsciously ask yourself to determine how effective you are at accomplishing your goals. And the way you answer that question is the difference between losing confidence and building it.

That magic question is: "How am I doing?"

Each time you take action to make something happen, whether it is in school, work, relationships, sports, or whatever or wherever you are doing it, you are receiving some kind of feedback in some form that tells you how effective you are in accomplishing the outcome you set out to create. The feedback you receive gives you the information that allows you to answer the question, "How am I doing?"

What are the sources of feedback in your life? Which people give you feedback? What things in your environment? How about your own thoughts?

What people and which thoughts are complimentary, critical, or complaining?

If you're clumsy like me, you get a lot of feedback from your environment—the crack in the sidewalk that trips you, the edge of the table you run into with your knee.

Perhaps you offer your own feedback in these moments in the form of colorful expletives.

In these moments, how do you answer the question, "How am I doing?"

Are you complimentary, critical, or complaining? Towards the environment or towards yourself?

What do you do to yourself when you use criticism to answer the question, "How am I doing?" In that moment, in that single answer to that one question, you chose to reinforce a feeling of incompetence.

In similar moments, we each have the opportunity to choose confidence or criticism. And this is the question that is always being asked and answered in the background of our minds all day long.

This is a question those with whom we are in relationships with answer as well. Their answers inform us how they think we're doing as a friend, spouse, parent, or coworker.

Now consider how many times a day someone asks you the question, "How are you doing?" as a greeting and you lie about it. "Fine," is the popular answer which you and I know actually means nothing but is simply a socially expected response to a rote greeting designed to answer the question so the conversation can get started.

If you're like me and answer honestly, you'll have moments like this: I get frequent chuckles when I go through the drive-through at a fast food restaurant and when asked, "Hi, welcome, how are you today?" I respond, "I'm hungry."

Sure, we get negative feedback from those around us but let's not forget all of the negative feedback we give ourselves. We enter adulthood with a toolbox overflowing with various options for beating ourselves up.

Have you ever had a hard day at work where you spent much of your eight-hour day getting nagged at by a colleague or chewed out by your boss, then you get home and your kid wants to run to you and give you a hug?

At that moment you find yourself uncomfortable with your child's positive energy or your spouse saying, "Glad you're home." In the past, I had days like that where the confidence was kicked out of me and I just couldn't handle any more input, let alone a compliment.

My kids, bless their hearts, are all waiting to see me with smiles and are glad I am home, but I cannot take compliments right then because it is very disproportionate to how I am feeling about myself at the time.

There are No Stupid Questions, Right?

"Take the attitude of a student: never be too big to ask questions, never know too much to learn something new."—Og Mandino

I learned of a teacher with the following classroom policy. "There's no such thing as a stupid question. So if you ever laugh at a fellow students' question I will give you a warning the first time and the second time, I'm kicking you out."

The moment I heard this I imagined how wonderful it would be if this policy were standard in every classroom. Now extend this policy to a work environment and imagine how it could positively impact collaboration. Let's explore this more.

When I shared this idea on a popular social network it started an interesting discussion when one teacher suggested that there is such a thing as a stupid question and that students need to be told that their questions are stupid.

She went on to say that she requires students to acknowledge their questions as stupid and explain to her why their questions were stupid. How's that for feedback?

Her efforts to defend this position suggested that in her mind, a stupid question is one in which she felt her time was being wasted. She also asserted students need to put more thought into questions before asking them.

Her final assertion was that lacking the distinction between stupid versus intelligent questions encourages intellectual laziness in students.

As expected, others in my online community shared their thoughts in response to her beliefs.

One parent stated, "I don't think telling children their questions are stupid is productive in any way whatsoever, and I would be horrified if one of my children came home upset because a teacher had said that to them. Teachers are supposed to nurture by building children up, not singling them out because they don't see or think the way the other kids might. It perpetuates bullying if you ask me."

Another parent shared, "My boys hardly ever participate because of fear of getting things wrong or being made to feel 'stupid.' I wish many more teachers took this particular teacher's approach then they would get far more interesting debates, all the pupils would learn to respect, everyone's point of view."

One of my favorite responses was, "Who decides what a stupid question is anyway? A question is valid whatever it is, surely teachers need to encourage children to think for themselves and not decide for them what sort of questions to ask."

Here's the comment I believe most gets to the heart of the matter, "When a teacher tells one pupil they have given a stupid answer, it doesn't exactly make it inviting for some of the more shy children to ask a question in the future, the more relaxed a child is the more likely the child can learn and even have fun doing so."

Final thoughts that were offered in this discussion were, "We encourage the students to engage. Especially the shy ones that have the question brewing but are too worried about the negative feedback from their peers. It is just one small way of creating an accepting classroom environment. Not one where the students judge one another."

One of my personal heroes is Socrates who is famous for asking questions. One of the most beautiful aspects of his approach was his relentless curiosity about the way others thought and how they reached the conclusions they did.

One lesson I took from Socrates' approach, that I believe is most relevant to this conversation, is that he welcomed all statements and all questions without judging the person making them or the question asked. Why?

He understood that only the free discussion of ideas allowed those exposed to them to learn from each other.

Granted, the rigors and strict requirements of the modern classroom make it difficult to have the long, intricate dialogues Socrates was used to, but I think there is plenty of room in the classroom and the boardroom for the spirit of inquiry.

The main value to be modeled in education is curiosity, and the wonder of discovery. The way both curiosity and wonder are satisfied are by asking questions.

The policy stated at the beginning of this conversation serves the purpose of making sure that curiosity and wonder are respected, embraced and supported.

In a world where too many kids are expected to sit still, be quiet, and do what they're told, I have the deepest respect for a teacher who prioritizes knowing what is on his/her students' minds.

Your Divided Attention, if You Please

"I have the attention span of a mosquito from multitasking and all the things that have affected my poor little brain."
—Ian Somerhalder

Light through a prism is very lovely, but it isn't the most effective use of light if you're trying to cut something. You need a laser, and the only way to achieve that is to focus the light so intensely that it can cut.

Our own attention is no different.

A phrase my boys hear from me on a nearly daily basis is, "Pick one." This occurs when I enter a room and find my oldest sitting in front of the computer with an iPhone in one hand and his Nintendo DS in the other, as well as my younger two who seem unable to watch TV and play their video games on their iTouches independent of each other.

On the surface they may appear skilled at multitasking but in reality what they're demonstrating is difficulty with sustained attention. They get bored quickly and want something readily available to move their attention to, over and over, to keep their minds stimulated.

How does this skill translate into interacting with another human being that needs your undivided attention? It doesn't.

Sometimes I feel like I need to be juggling flaming chainsaws while belching Gangnam Style just to keep their attention.

I'll admit I'm not always the best at focusing when I need to, but when I am focused I invite the boys to join me there. Relationships are the most important thing in this life and if we can't attend to the person in front of us they'll know it and what our diffused attention will tell them is that something else is more important than they are.

The way I invite my boys to join me in the moment is by letting them know where my focus is.

For example, I'll be in the middle of working on my computer and my oldest Zach will interrupt me by asking, "What are you doing?" I'll take a moment to stop what I'm doing, take a deep breath, shift my intention, then turn to him and reply, "Talking to you."

He'll clarify, "No, what are you doing on the computer?" To which I say, "That's what I was doing. What I AM doing is talking to you."

Yesterday we were running errands, only a few of which the boys were aware of. I decided to throw in a few surprises. While en route to one of them, Zach asked, "Where are we going now?" I pointed straight ahead and said, "That way."

This was an opportunity for him to be reminded that our time together includes the journey as well as the destination.

I was particularly impressed with Zach one day when he demonstrated that this lesson was truly sinking in. Our family decided to explore a forest preserve we'd never been to before and I got ahead of myself. I envisioned a spacious area with trees as far as the eye could see, a creek, and multiple paths for walking.

Alas, this one turned out to be quite simple. One pond, one path, mostly grass, and a few trees. While I silently fretted, Zach remained mindful as we walked to the end of the one path and back again. When he asked me what I thought of the forest preserve I noted my unfulfilled expectations to which Zach quickly replied, "But we had a nice walk didn't we?"

I smiled. It's the moments in which my son teaches me that my responsibilities as a parent are truly realized.

You have Permission to Learn

"Write yourself a permission slip to be surprised by someone's potential. Who knows? One day that person could be you."
—Sherri Shepherd

During a conversation with a group of parents and educators, one person remarked that parents need to give themselves permission to allow their children to fail.

I took it a step further and suggested that instead of failure it would be more useful to give them permission to learn.

So many parents and educators alike unintentionally model the importance of being right, or being perfect and scold children for not knowing what they're expected to know the moment they're expected to know it.

Too often in life we believe that only the desired outcome is worth something when, in fact, every experience has value.

It reminds me of a story I heard about a martial arts master who was instructing two students as they participated in full-contact sparring. They each took turns giving and receiving strikes.

When the master announced that they had done enough and could finish for the day, one student inquired, "Master, which one of us won?"

"What do you mean?" The master questioned.

"Doesn't one of us have to win and the other one lose?" The student clarified.

To which the master replied, "Is it not more important what you choose to do with either outcome?"

The lesson is that it isn't about winning or losing, it's always about learning.

When it comes to parenting, educating, or leading in a company, the one that learns the most is the one who is most teachable.

I learned early on that needing to be right, and feeling as though I needed to have all the answers, led to me feeling inadequate much of the time. It also modeled for my children that being right was more of a virtue than being teachable.

One day, I decided to give myself permission to be a student, to be curious again and experience the world alongside my children.

With curiosity there is no failure because everything is a discovery, after which we can ask ourselves the same question, "What did we discover from this?"

With that approach, defeat never enters the conversation; there's no need to punish ourselves in order to learn the valuable lessons life has to teach us.

You have permission to find the answers; there's no need to always have them.

You have permission to trust; trust that each lesson will require you to grow.

You have permission to fall, so the muscles required to get back up become the strongest of all.

I'm Naming my Son after You

"Don't wish me happiness—I don't expect to be happy, it's gotten beyond that, somehow. Wish me courage and strength and a sense of humor—I will need them all."—Anne Morrow Lindbergh

Do you have a memory from your childhood, of an elder relative, who for even a moment was a hero to you?

That would be my Grandpa Bodony, my mother's father.

Through one of the most difficult periods of my life, he always reminded me that he believed in me, that I was strong, that I could do it.

My grandpa emigrated with his parents from Romania when he was 3 years old. He lived through the Great Depression and with his wife, Emily, raised seven children, six sons and one daughter, my mother.

The grandpa I knew was the old man in his recliner, the man who always greeted me with a smile and a firm handshake.

I remember how proud I was as I grew in years and in strength, the measure of which was to match Grandpa's handshake. My goal was to be as strong as the man I so looked forward to seeing.

It was as though when he shook my hand firmly, inviting me to match him, he was encouraging me to be stronger.

Then came the most difficult period of my life, the summer after high school graduation during which I battled cancer.

I remember going to family gatherings, walking in with my bald head (then as a result of the chemotherapy) and my baseball cap on. I remember overhearing my relatives talk about me, instead of to me.

"How's he doing?" they'd whisper to my mother, never talking to me directly.

Then there was Grandpa. The moment he saw me, his face would light up and he'd grab my hand and invite me to join him in the firm handshake we'd been practicing all my life. And as we shook hands, he'd look me in the eye and say, "How yah doin', boy, you look great, you're doing great, you can do this."

I believed him.

On a few of my better days when I felt a little stronger and not quite as nauseous, I would drive to my grandpa's house to spend a few hours with him.

I'd sit as he tended his garden, offered me bits of wisdom, and gave me the respect, the time and attention that others in the family found it difficult to give, for whatever reason.

I remember one day in particular: it was sunny, warm, and beautiful as was Grandpa's disposition. I looked to him and said, "You know what, if I ever have a son, I'm going to name him after you."

"Why, thank you." he responded, with a surprised look on his face. I went on to explain to him how valuable his support of me had been, how fatherly he'd been to me, and how his example inspired me to do likewise for my son.

Though it was a short exchange between Grandpa and me, as far as I was concerned, I had made him a promise.

Later my doctors told me that I may never have children due to the chemotherapy, and it broke my heart on so many levels. One of which was the thought that I might not be able to keep my promise to my grandpa.

Many years later I met and eventually married my then-wife Katie and three months into our marriage learned she was pregnant. Take that, doctors!

When an ultrasound revealed it was a boy, I sat down with Katie and told her of my promise to my grandfather. She, of course, supported it 100%.

Then, on January 1, 1998 our son, Zachary Vasile King was born. I gave him my grandfather's Romanian first name as his middle name. Sadly, Grandpa died many years before Zach was born, but I know he was looking down and smiling.

When Zach was old enough, I told him of those special moments I had had with my grandfather. How those moments taught me the power of caring for someone else—of being strong in a way that you can invite someone else to be strong with you, when you find it difficult to uncover the strength in yourself.

Grandpa taught me about strength, through something as simple as a handshake, something as simple as his belief in my strength and his willingness to be there, with me, when I most needed it.

For my boys, I will always do the same. Thank you, Grandpa.

It All Happened at Once

"We can't help everyone, but everyone can help someone."
—Ronald Reagan

Some will begin this day with a sense of dread for what is to come.

Still others will begin it with a sense of gratitude for everything that has helped them come this far, and for their opportunity to pay it forward.

One weekend was a real humdinger for my family.

Friday evening, my boys went to go spend the weekend with their mother (my ex) and had a great deal of fun planned.

Saturday morning my ex called. She had received an urgent phone call to come to her mother's apartment. Upon arriving she was informed her mother had died. She requested that my wife, Cathy, and I meet her later to support our boys together when they received the news. This was the first death they'd experienced, and the first time we as parents would share this experience with them.

As Cathy and I were getting ready to leave the house we received a call from a relative who was in a financial bind and humbly asked if we were in a financial position to help. We were. It also turns out that this same relative extended a hand of generosity when we were in a similar situation.

We arrived at my ex's home and gathered the boys together. We began by reminding them that Nana had been sick for a while and then informed them that earlier in the morning she had passed away. Our seven-year-old expressed that he didn't know what that meant. I told him it meant she died. I added that she was asleep when it happened so she was comfortable when it happened.

There was some anger, many tears, and as many hugs as they needed. We had a conversation about death, spirits and the afterlife that appeared to lend some comfort.

Overall, they handled it much better than we had expected. It's amazing how resilient children can be.

I woke up early the next morning having planned to sleep in. However, I was so restless from the previous day's events that sleep wasn't easy to come by, so I woke up and read. It was very relaxing.

Cathy and I spent a quiet morning together, went to breakfast and ran errands before the boys were to arrive home.

While running errands I received a call from another relative. This relative explained that their troubled marriage had resulted in the sudden decision to separate.

I listened quietly, and then offered any support that I could.

That night Cathy and I looked to each other and wondered what the hell this was all about. Why so much at once? What was going on?

You know me—I refuse to frame even weekends such as this as an indication that the world is going to hell, bad things happen in threes etc.

Instead, I reflected on it and said, "Thank you." I expressed gratitude for the fact that we were able to help.

All my life there were countless moments where I was down and needed to rely on the strength of others coupled with my own to get back up.

Others extended their hand and helped me up. This weekend others extended their hand to us and asked, "Will you help me up?"

This weekend was a reminder of one of life's greatest truths— We're all in this together. We need each other.

Sometimes we need the help, sometimes we give the help. Together we keep moving forward, because we keep paying forward all of the times we were helped.

Who Matters to You?

"Appreciation is a wonderful thing: It makes what is excellent in others belong to us as well."—Voltaire

Did you ever experience a moment when you really felt appreciated by someone?

What did he do? Was it a smile while saying, "Thank you," or a simple pat on your back?

What did the person do or say that led to the thought or feeling that, "Hey, this person really likes me. This person really enjoys my company. I really matter to this person."

I think that much of what motivates me is remembering how it felt as a kid, when it seemed the whole world was against me and then someone took the time to care.

I remember being on the receiving end of that and how powerful those moments were. Moments I now make a point of helping create for others.

Knowing what it feels like to be on the receiving end of those expressions of appreciation and after reflecting upon exactly what someone said or did to help you create that moment, imagine how powerful a tool that is.

Imagine making a deliberate effort to do and say the things that help you and someone else experience a moment of appreciate together.

Now imagine how much fuller your day and your life would be if you did this a lot. Are you smiling just thinking about it? I am.

Try it out and let me know what happens.

How to Give Valuable Advice to Friends and Family

"When a man comes to me for advice, I find out the kind of advice he wants, and I give it to him."—*Josh Billings*

Unsolicited advice is one of the biggest pet peeves for many people.

Was there a recent time when either a good friend or a member of your family made one of the following statements, "Here's what you should do," "Well, if I were you..."

Was there a recent time when you uttered one of those phrases and the result was being snapped at, when all you were trying to do was help?

There is a lot of good advice out there that never gets heard, simply because it is unsolicited.

One of the best things about communication is our right, our option, and our ability to negotiate how it's done in our relationships.

YES, we can actually agree to how we talk with each other and one of the most important agreements to make is how to advise each other.

When you have advice you feel would be helpful and not simply serve the purpose of hearing yourself talk (very important distinction to make before opening your mouth),

177

you could ask ..."I have some experience with this and have a suggestion that might be helpful, would you like to hear it?"

You'll get a YES, a NO, or a "Not right now" answer.

Sometimes a person is still processing the issue and even though you may have identified what *you* believe the problem to be, the person in question hasn't yet.

The key is that you've offered yourself as a resource, so when the time is right and the person is ready, they have the option to seek you out. She doesn't have the obligation to seek you out or to implement your advice, for that matter.

What matters is that you have now set up a scenario where you will be asked for advice when it has the greatest likelihood of being valuable.

Here's a recap:

1) Get permission to offer advice.

2) Clarify to make sure you're both defining the problem to be solved the same way.

3) Be grateful for the opportunity to be helpful, whether s/he applies your advice or not.

You Need Something to Depend on, Right?

"I can count on one hand how many people I trust." —*Frances Bean Cobain*

We all need something we can count on in our lives. The one constant that gives us something to hold on to, as we navigate this world, moves from variations of simple surprise, significant uncertainty, and often (what feels like) unbridled chaos.

I've known people who need to wear a certain piece of jewelry, wear their lucky hat, have a photo in their wallet, or carry some other object at all times, or they become extremely anxious.

For them, it provides a constant—a connection to an event or a person that helps them tap into the feeling of confidence that they need to get through a difficult situation.

At various times throughout my life I've carried lucky coins, a positive saying on a strip of paper in my wallet that I'd look at daily, and other various objects. The main importance they had for me wasn't that they were lucky. It was because I could count on them being there. I could count on looking in my wallet for my lucky coin and it would be there.

Sometimes, it's so you're never alone.

If you saw the movie "Castaway" with Tom Hanks, you'll remember that he created a companion from a volleyball he named Wilson. He went so far as to protect Wilson as though it were another person.

179

That brings me to Thumper— you know, the rabbit from Bambi. Thumper helped guide Bambi (who was shy and vulnerable) in the ways of the forest. He served as a guide, showing Bambi the ropes.

In the spring of 1988, I was diagnosed with testicular cancer (I was 18 years old). I spent the summer in chemotherapy. The first week was spent at Indiana University Medical center (I'm from the suburbs of Chicago), where the world's leading specialist was. My life was turned upside-down and inside out.

The first week was pure hell. Some time in those first few days my mother was poking through the hospital gift shop and found Thumper. She bought him for me and twenty-five years later, he's still with me. Now he sits atop my desk.

Thumper was with me through every day in the hospital during chemo, he was with me at home when I was feeling miserable. He is soft, comfortable, snugly and has that adorable little face that makes me smile every time I look at him.

For those of us struggling to make our way through this complex world, it is often the little things we need to hold onto that help keep us focused and keep us going. Sometimes it seems that without those things, we'd be lost.

Do you have a Thumper in your life? If not, I highly recommend getting one.

The six treasures of friendship

"You are the average of the five people you spend the most time with."—Jim Rohn

Friendships are uniquely powerful in how they shape our lives and how they shape who we become.

Let's begin with a question. If I wanted to be an awesome friend to you, what would I need to do? Take some time to really think about this. Do you have clear criteria for who gets to be your friend and who doesn't?

Once you have your criteria, you need to find people that satisfy those criteria, right? For once you find the right person who values what you value, the way you value it, then that is a person you'll likely feel very connected to.

As you talk with him, get to know him, spend time with him, you'll be on a hunt for that information, those little golden nuggets that connect you.

In order to be an awesome friend, you must first and foremost be a treasurer hunter, because what are you looking for? You're looking for those little pearls, those little pieces of gold, those little diamonds in the rough, those things that are unique to the person who you are inviting into your life to be your friend, and you want to share those things with them.

After all, you'll be giving each other the most precious thing anybody on the planet earth can ever give you, and what is

181

that? Your time and attention. Nobody can give you anybody else's time; it's yours to give.

Now, as a treasure hunter, what do you think a treasure hunt consists of?

Do you expect to find treasure the first time you dig? Of course not! Well, what do you expect to find? Dirt, right?

So does that mean life is unfair, life stinks, so we should just go home and hide under the covers? No!

When you put yourself out there, trying to meet people, there will be many who are impolite, selfish, or simply not a good fit. This is a fact and not a cause to give up talking to anyone ever again.

You're a treasure hunter, and you know there's going to be a lot of dirt, there's going to be some rock, and there's going to be some fools gold. It may look like gold at first, but it's not. The equivalent of that in a relationship would be somebody who pretends to be your friend, seem nice on the surface, but then something happens, she talks about you behind your back, or she's mean to you in front of her friends because she wants to impress them.

Do you expect to find fool's gold in a treasure hunt? Yes, and as disappointing as those moments are, is your life over? What do you do? You keep hunting.

You have gotten this far in life for the simple reason that you have persevered. You're a treasure hunter. You are in search of those special moments, those special people that have those little treasurers within them. The unique gifts only they have that they are willing, ready, and able to share with you. People whose generosity you can repay by returning the favor, because they are on a treasure hunt looking for you.

What kind of experiences do you look for in an awesome friendship?

Memories: "Do you remember the time when?" "I'll never forget when we did that." It's those moments you're creating together, those moments have value. They change your life into a forward direction; they pull you forward into greater things.

Let's talk about how you do that... how do you create those moments? In my experience, when you're treasure hunting, there are six main treasures of friendship; Tony Robbins refers to them as the six human needs. In the greatest of friendships, every one of these treasures is there.

The first one is certainty. People need to be certain of you; they need to know they can count on you, that they can trust you. So you must be consistent, you must have integrity. If you say, you're going to do it you better do it. If you say you're going to show up, you better be there unless you're in the hospital. That is certainty.

If you don't have that kind of certainty in your friendships right now, require it. Hold yourself and the people in your life to a higher standard, because too many people settle in their relationships.

Too many allow others to treat them like dirt and then say, oh, it's okay, it happens sometimes and you know what you've just given them the green light to do? Do it again. You teach people how to treat you like garbage.

If you require trust, you require integrity; the people who value that, too, will show up in your life, because they're tired of being stabbed in the back as well–that's a certainty. Do you agree? That's the first treasure.

The second treasure is variety. Variety refers to the new and different things another person brings to your life, as well as the fun and excitement. If someone comes along and says, "I'm bored, what do you want to do?" Hangout?" That's not variety. If someone says, let's try something new today; let's have an adventure, somewhere we haven't gone yet, exploring new things, new opportunities, learning together. That's variety.

The third treasure is significance, and it is found in every moment that the person you're with reminds you that you matter. They matter more to you than anybody else in the world right now. Why? Because what are you giving them? Your time and attention. You're not checking your email, you're not texting someone, you're not thinking about what you're doing the rest of the day, you're right here, right now... with the person in front of you.

You don't have to say any magic words, you don't have to tell them how pretty they look, how nice their outfit is, just be there and care. That's a powerful principle for life, be there and care that's how you show someone else they are significant. When they give you the same back, they remind you that you matter, too.

How hard is it to just be there and give someone your undivided attention? It's not hard, is it? It's not hard at all. It's that easy to show someone that they matter in this world.

The fourth treasure is connection, those little things that only we share together—the things that are uniquely ours. Most people believe there are only two people in a relationship. There's you and there's me, but there's one more, and it's the most important one. It's we, our partnership, our relationship, and our bond that nobody else has. It's just ours and we created it together, that's our connection.

The fifth treasure is growth, because a friendship that meets your needs will never leave you in the same place it found you. It will always make more of you.

Making mistakes together is a wonderful way to grow. Mistakes happen in teachable moments, in human moments. You need to be able to be human beings together.

Through your ability to be safe and vulnerable together, you also discover you have the potential to be stronger than you imagined you could be. A friend will encourage you to be as great as he thinks you are.

The sixth treasure is contribution. Contribution is showing up every day, being of service, thinking about how you are going to add value to someone else's world. What of yourself are you going to contribute to someone else?

Let's review the six treasures:

Certainty

Variety

Significance

Connection

Growth

Contribution

You can practice them all immediately. You will change lives in more profound ways than you realize beginning with your own. Because, ultimately, what you're creating and manifesting by finding and practicing these six treasures is a compelling story—the story of your life, the story of your friendship.

When two friends reach out to hug each other what's between them? A small space, right?

Do you know what that space consists of? Everything you put there, that is the third party. That's the "we", which is your story, that space is what you're creating together. Every time you think about that space, ask yourself, "What am I putting in there?"

Every time you're with your friend, your parent, your brother, your sister, you are adding to the story of their life, you're adding to the story of your friendship, of your relationship... what are you going to put there?

So when you're telling your story and you're remembering those moments that you have with that person, "I remember the time when, "I'll never forget when we did that." Make it a compelling story that's filled with certainty and variety, significance, growth, love, connection, contribution.

Make it a story of a changed life, a life that is transformed because you took the time, because you gave your attention that's what a friendship is. That's what life is about, the story of our journey together, the story of our friendships.

Now go out and change somebody's world.

Work

There is no "I" in "We"

"Coming together is a beginning; keeping together is progress; working together is success."—Henry Ford

There are two main questions you must answer for yourself before you can build the life you want.

1) What kind of relationship(s) do I want for myself?

2) What am I willing to give in return for it?

The quality of our life depends upon the quality of our relationships, NOT the quantity of them.

Do you see relationships as competitive —win/lose?

Are they cooperative—win/win?

Does it matter? Why?

Those who have the biggest trouble in relationships are those who have too many "I" statements in their description of it.

Someone who does all the talking and complains that, "You never listen to me." Hmmmm... how can your partner listen when she/he doesn't know what it feels like to be listened to?

The most fulfilling relationships are motivated by finding out what needs you have in common and what the best ways are for meeting them together.

Relationships are not transaction-based; it's not about keeping score of how many compliments or how many times you have sex during the week.

Relationships are about the journey you've agreed to have together, the experiences you want to share and agree to co-create. It's about being present with the person you're with regardless of what experience you're having at the time.

Don't expect anything from another person that you aren't willing to give first. You are the best one to demonstrate what it means to you to be held, touched, supported, and loved.

There is a sacred space between you and every other person on the planet. What you put in that space, nurture, and replenish, is what grows.

That space is the relationship itself, the synergy that only exists because of your mutual efforts. Your side of the bargain consists of what you decide to put in the space that we share, and that connects us. The quality of the connection is determined by the quality of what each of us adds to the space.

Perfect moments arise when we both add trust at the same time, vulnerability in the same moment.

The reality is that far too often we put stubbornness in this space! We put arrogance in this space. We put impatience in this space.

We end up building walls instead of doors, cutting ties instead of strengthening the ones already there.

The key is to be mindful of when we do this so that we can choose instead to put listening in this space, along with compassion and patience in this space, so the wall will come crumbling down and transform into a foundation for stronger connection.

When you focus on nurturing that space, you are asking yourself the very important questions, "Are we building a wall or a path?" "What in this situation could be working better?" "What will help us feel more connected?" Focusing on "we" instead of "me" places your attention more on the partnership, where it needs to be when the two of you are together.

Too much time spent thinking of one of you over the other one drains that space of the energy needed to grow.

When you think of both parties equally, your language changes from "You're doing this wrong" to "What's not working here? What can work better?" That simple shift in your focus is, usually, "the million dollar shift".

It is exactly what it takes to go from "I'm not getting anywhere with you" to "It feels like we've really grown here." "It feels like we're really hearing each other."

It usually does not take a massive reorganization of your life, your psyche, and who you are to move beyond yourself in order to connect with others. It just takes those little shifts.

Making these little shifts is important, but becoming aware enough to know which shifts to make is something I refer to as the "effective factor." I want to point out that the effective factor isn't something I created, it's something I noticed. It's something that's just part of how life works.

Here's a simple example of this point. On a particularly hot summer day, I noticed some flowers my wife had recently planted had wilted. I knew that many factors go into helping a flower thrive. Factors such as soil and sunlight, both of which the flower had plenty of and yet it was wilting.

So in this case I needed to identify the one factor that would make the greatest difference in this moment between continuing to wilt and begin to thrive again. The effective factor was water.

The flowers perked back up within minutes of being watered. The flowers were now able to make greater use of the sun and the soil. The flowers were able to be more resourceful.

The effective factor is one of those rules of the universe that if you understand how it works and you apply it consistency, you can get the positive results.

A Simple Way to be More Happy Today

"Happiness in the present is only shattered by comparison with the past."—Douglas Horton

I was having a conversation with a friend, which began in typical fashion with my asking the question, "How's your day so far?"

His response was, "Not as productive as I'd like it to be. Ya know, I got a late start and was able to get some things done, but not everything I wanted to get done." He added, "Overall, I can't complain."

"I can't complain" is a statement that is focusing on the absence of a negative instead of the presence of a positive.

Sure you can't complain, but it's also difficult to find gratitude for the progress you've made and enjoy it while your focus is on what didn't go as planned.

I explained this to him and he said. "Good point."

I added that the root of human suffering is dissatisfaction. Which means that when you judge any given moment as "not good enough", you suffer to some degree because you're emphasizing what is lacking, instead of what is present.

As human beings, we are very good at removing the joy from our experiences by comparing them to what "could've been" or "should've been" and by belittling the value of what is.

I'm not suggesting that we don't strive to improve our circumstances by being more present-minded; I'm suggesting that we learn to do it in a way that emphasizes the abundance of what's present, instead of the scarcity, lack, or fixating on what's missing.

Here's a recommendation for being positively present.

However things go in the course of your day, you will at some point compare how it's going to the ideal you had in mind when your day started.

Instead of making a comment such as, "Well, it isn't as productive as I would've liked."

You can instead say, "Look at how productive I've been." Then add, "Now what would I have to do to be even more productive?"

The second statement doesn't suggest your present level of productivity isn't good enough; it celebrates your productivity and sees it as something to build upon.

It isn't expected that you'll be able to do this 100% of the time. I don't. The key is to be aware of this tendency, so you can catch yourself more often than not and quickly shift your thinking.

You can then take more of those moments back for yourself and experience the joy that is there by celebrating a job well done, even if it wasn't the ideal.

There's nothing broken, there's nothing missing, because there's only you creating the best results you can in this moment. Results that lay the perfect foundation for everything that is to come.

To Be BLUNT or Not to Be

"Take advantage of every opportunity to practice your communication skills so that when important occasions arise, you will have the gift, the style, the sharpness, the clarity, and the emotions to affect other people."—Jim Rohn

"I'm blunt, that's just the way I am and if you don't like it you can just take a flying leap."

This statement was made by someone I've come to know as believing that thinking before speaking is a waste of time. This person went on to say that bluntness is "a part of who I am."

That last statement is the beginning of the problem.

There is a misunderstanding in the mind of many people in which they mistake their style for their identity.

Bluntness is a style, as is diplomacy, something I've learned to master over the years because my bluntness alienated so many people.

I didn't change my style to be someone else; I changed it because it's a more effective way of connecting with people. It's the difference between greeting people with a fist or a handshake.

It's like someone saying, "I'm just stubborn," or " "I'm just an angry person." When something begins with "I am" you're telling yourself that these traits are inseparable from you.

That's baloney. Clearly there will be times when you are flexible instead of stubborn, happy instead of angry, yes? Then "stubborn" and "angry" aren't you.

Then, who are you? (Drumroll please).

You are the pattern of beliefs and values that you prioritize at this moment. And everything you say and do is driven by them, period. End of story.

When I realized that the way I perceive the world is based on a pattern of beliefs and values, I realized I could change my view of the world by changing the pattern I was using. I wasn't changing ME. I was changing the pattern.

If I wanted different results in my relationships, I needed to change my pattern of beliefs and values about the way I decided relationships needed to work. This also changed my beliefs about what I could and couldn't do.

THAT'S IT, FOLKS! That's what it boils down to: Change the pattern and change the results.

It the end, you'll experience life more fully than you ever have before.

How do we Understand Each Other?

"Don't make assumptions. Find the courage to ask questions and to express what you really want. Communicate with others as clearly as you can to avoid misunderstandings, sadness, and drama. With just this one agreement, you can completely transform your life."—Miguel Angel Ruiz

Within the past several years I discovered that decoding nonverbal communication was not my strong suit and yet those in my life use it regularly. In my effort to connect with them I had to find strategies for creatively bypassing this challenge of mine in order to understand them anyway.

An important thing I realized through this process is that I didn't need to learn how to understand all of the nonverbal communication being thrown my way; I just needed to know that it was occurring and I was missing it.

In addition to discovering what I miss, I have found that a serious blind spot in the self-awareness of many is what they miss when communicating with others. People will defend their perception by saying, "I heard what you said, and I know exactly what you meant." That assertion is rarely accurate.

In my experience we often miss more than we catch. To realize this fact alone dramatically improves communication because it compels you to clarify your understanding with whomever you're communicating.

I have learned to clarify by asking questions in order to encourage a person to verbalize, or in some other concrete way, express what they're communicating nonverbally.

Let's define *clarification* so we understand it in the same way. *Clarification* is checking in with the person you are communicating with, in order to verify the message you received is the message the other person intended. The reverse is true as well.

For this purpose, only a verbal or very well-written response will do. There is simply no point in requiring one person to guess what the other person is thinking. Always ask.

An important role of clarification is establishing the way you agree to communicate with each other. Let's define *communication* as a process of sharing information using an agreed-upon method such as speaking, writing, texting, e-mailing, or signing. And it is following agreed upon rules of exchange.

In addition to the means of communication, what manner of communication is allowed? Are there things that must take place, e.g. saying "please" and "thank you"? Are there things that mustn't take place, such as swearing or lying?

Remember, clarification is a two-way street. Both people in a relationship need to agree to use it for it to work.

Clarification is the most important communication strategy in any partnership, as far as I'm concerned. Many people claim to value clarifying, but hardly anybody does it. If they do it, it tends to be inconsistent.

Most of the people I've met understand clarification as a concept, but they haven't taken the time to define it in a functional way and they've never learned it as a concrete, deliberate strategy.

If you say that you clarify all the time, well, maybe you clarify some of the time, but I guarantee that you do not clarify as often as you need to. For instance, have you ever experienced misunderstandings, arguments, or misperceptions in your relationships?

How often after a misunderstanding, do you think to yourself, "Oh, well, next time I'll remember to ask or check in with him/her," and then you don't? This is because you haven't learned to believe clarification is critical, a priority, or essential. That is why you don't do it enough.

In my life, I miss so much nonverbal information that I'd better clarify so that I have enough information to know what the heck is going on, and by doing so, my life has become so much easier.

There is one glitch when it comes to both people agreeing to clarify with one another on a regular basis. The glitch is that people generally resist clarifying and often are socially trained not to.

When attempting to clarify, have you ever received responses such as, "You should have been paying attention," or "You should have listened the first time."

If you have ever responded this way, then understand that what you've done is criticize someone for clarifying with you. Do parents ever do this to their children, teachers with their students, or supervisors with their staff?

Have you ever heard, "I don't like repeating myself"?

When someone gives you an opportunity to be better understood by clarifying and you become defensive, what do you teach them about clarifying with you? Not to do it because it makes you mad.

I made a point of doing a little research among my peers and asked them whether they resisted clarifying. Those who answered yes were also able to explain why.

The first reason is that many people think their perception is "spot-on" and that they get it right the first time. I call this the curse of immaculate perception. Those people still have a lot of miscommunication and misunderstandings because they do not question their own perception.

Even though they are proven incorrect time and time again, it doesn't occur to them to do anything different. Even worse is when they blame the other person for the miscommunication.

There is even a word that describes the habit of thinking you got it right, don't need to clarify, and believe you have enough information without it. The word is assumption.

People rely more on assumption than clarification, even though it is incredibly unreliable. Unreliable because assumption requires mind-reading; it is guessing. There is no information-gathering in assumption.

Assumption is the false belief that communication has taken place without any proof. This is dangerous in a relationship and yet we all do it. I have done it myself and I am working diligently to do it less and less. People assume that they know what the other person meant, how the other person feels, and worst of all, they believe they know what the other person is thinking.

Assuming you know what is going on in someone's internal life is the most absurd assumption. It makes more sense to learn how to diplomatically ask what another person is thinking. Don't read a person's mind; ask him a question and clarify.

Assumption causes many misunderstandings and resolves none of them.

Have you assumed things while communicating, and if so, what were the results of having done so? Sure, you might get it right on occasion. You might be working with somebody who you know very well, who is very predictable and relatively easy to read. Being able to read *some* people so well lulls you into a false sense of security.

Now, think about the other person who assumes you understood him and, when there's a misunderstanding, blames you as though understanding was solely your responsibility.

The problem was in the assumption and the fact that the clarification did not take place. Wouldn't it make more sense to clarify and make sure you understood him or for him to make sure he was understood by you? Ask the questions, get the clarification, and you will not have to worry about it.

I've repeatedly encountered a statistic that states nonverbal communication accounts for well over eighty-five percent of communication. If that is correct, we are all in big trouble and the reason why that is that because it means we are not talking to each other.

We instead rely on hints, innuendos, and suggestions so that we don't *have* to talk to each other. I don't believe that over eighty-five percent of communication must be nonverbal, I believe it's our bodies communicating what we're afraid to talk about or don't know how to talk about.

It isn't that we can't make a greater percentage of our communication verbal; it's that we don't.

Nonverbal may give you some hints as to what a person is feeling but it does not tell you for certain. It's important to ask, "Is there more I need to know that you haven't told me?" That invites the person to tell me if he wants me to know it.

I could easily assume he's told me everything, walk away, have a misunderstanding, and blame him for not being clear enough in the first place.

Again, overestimating your own perception and <u>assuming</u> is the first reason people don't clarify. A bigger reason people do not clarify, as I mentioned earlier, is the fear the other person will be angry with them.

Are you afraid of asking the wrong questions, sounding too pushy, sounding rude, and that someone else will be angry with you? So much, in fact, that you will risk miscommunication and misunderstanding just to avoid their anger?

The reality is that all you really accomplish by not clarifying at the time is postponing anger. You can ask now and maybe the other person will get upset with you, or you can walk away trusting your perception only to find out later you misunderstood and find he/she is angry with you because you misunderstood. Does that make sense?

What's worse is that the one strategy, clarification, is something we're taught from childhood to avoid doing. We learned the worst thing we could do is make someone else angry, and as a parent, I admit, I was guilty of this, too, at one point.

Your children do things to push your buttons and you react by saying, "Don't make me angry!" It is the ultimate warning. What happens is we are teaching our children that our anger is their responsibility. So, it is their responsibility to not make us angry, even if it's at the expense of clarifying. Spend time thinking about that.

It's unfortunate when clarification does result in an angry response, especially from you. If you respond this way often enough people will begin protecting themselves by telling you what they think you want to hear.

In order to be able to make clarification a priority in your relationships, you need to have a belief about clarification that makes it a priority. By *belief*, I don't mean simply thinking that clarification is a good idea.

A belief is something you feel, and when you don't do what you believe, you feel extremely uncomfortable. If it's simply a good idea, you may forget it and not notice. But when you go against a belief, you know it.

The belief that reinforces valuing clarification is, "I must be certain I know what a person is thinking or feeling, and the only way to be certain is by asking." Certainty isn't possible when assuming.

When you must be certain, and you trust nothing else except asking, you will be compelled to ask. You understand that your perception is imperfect and that the only way you will know is to clarify.

With this belief, when you see someone who appears happy, you'll realize she might be happy but you don't know and won't be sure until you clarify. So, you have a belief that says, "I don't have enough information until I ask. If I haven't asked, I don't know. I'm guessing and some people unfortunately mistake guessing and assumptions for knowledge." That is where misunderstanding occurs.

This is how I clarify a facial expression: "You seem to be happy about something, is that right?

"Isn't it obvious?"

"Just making sure. It would be disrespectful for me to think that I know what you are thinking or what you are feeling and that is why I am asking."

Do you always have to ask how a person is feeling or thinking? The answer is you don't always have to ask, but make sure that if you choose not to ask, that what you perceive is an assumption and not fact until you clarify.

Don't make the mistake of deciding something without the clarification that gives you enough information to decide. All right....

So how do you agree to clarify in a relationship with a person who has "immaculate perception"?

Model it for him with statements such as, "I heard you say that you think you know what I'm thinking. Well, the fact is I don't know what you're thinking. When I say something to you, I don't know how you're going to respond so I don't always choose the perfect words. I choose the words I can think of, then I need you to tell me what you think I meant so I can give you more words to explain what I really meant until I've used enough words for us to understand each other."

Now I know that sounds complex, but think more about the spirit of the statement. You want to explain to him that mind-reading isn't a skill of yours, and it takes a few times to get all of the words out that help you best get your point across. Does that help?

We need the awareness of how our minds work in a social situation—what information we perceive and what we miss. Then, make a point of learning how to get that information through clarifying instead of reading unreliable nonverbal cues.

We both want to be understood, but we must be flexible in how we get the information we need from each other.

We need to emphasize the product over the process. I've become who I am today through negotiating my relationships in terms of what we need from each other, not from making myself into someone I'm not to make the other person happy at my expense.

A very specific and helpful use for clarification is when you find yourself in new surroundings. Your new boyfriend or girlfriend invites you to meet the parents. A colleague invites you to lunch with a few associates and you'd like to know about any specific expectations beforehand.

You can ask one of several questions to get the information you need, "Excuse me, how is this supposed to go?" "What is my role here?" "What would you like me to do?" "Are there things you usually talk or don't talk about?"

Keep in mind; I have spent upwards of twenty years thinking this through, so this may make much more sense in my head. I devote my time to figuring out how to make communication more effective without it being a source of pain for me or the other person.

How do you know when you've clarified enough? When you're both satisfied that you understand what action is to be taken, based on the conversation.

You would ask, "Based on what you said, I'm hearing that you want me to do this in this way. Is that correct?" When the other person confirms your understanding of the action you'll take, then you have complete clarification.

Constructive Criticism Isn't

When it comes to our relationships we need to spend more time on "connection" instead of "correction."—Brian R. King

A myth I continue to hear promoted, especially in academic and corporate settings, is the idea of constructive criticism. Are there any bigger oxymorons than that? Constructive criticism—what do you think of that term? What, if any, issues do you have with the term *constructive criticism*?

I think of constructive criticism as well-intended negative feedback. It is like calling someone a fat slob and then saying you don't mean it in a bad way. You are basically trying to cover up an insult. So, what is the alternative?

Constructive criticism is intended by most people as a means of giving guidance for improving upon what could be done better. Is this accurate?

The problem with constructive criticism is it comes out as, "Here is what you are doing wrong, and here is how to do it better." You are leading with a negative or leading in with the fault. So here's the alternative I use with my own children, clients, and colleagues.

This is one of my best strategies. You can eliminate the criticism altogether, and the tendency for the person to take it personally, by offering feedback about how the situation is going instead of how the person is doing.

Instead of asking, "Are you having a problem?" you ask, "Is something not working?"

A person who is used to hearing criticism may initially hear it as personal and may respond something like, "I'm fine, I don't need any help."

But remember, with this approach, you're not asking about the person, you're asking about the aspect of the situation that isn't working.

So when he says, "I'm fine, I don't need any help," you respond, "Oh, I'm sure you're doing fine. I was wondering if something in this situation wasn't going the way it needs to go."

This small adjustment can take the responsibility or the fault away from the person and make it about the situation. It is much easier to hear feedback when the negative is not aimed at him.

You want to build confidence and build opportunities for problem solving. But the moment you say there is a problem and that he caused it, he may not want any more feedback from you.

One concern that's been expressed about this approach is whether it allows someone to dodge responsibility for his actions. The answer is no.

My approach emphasizes that a specific approach to the situation is the issue not a problem with the person himself. Therefore by examining and perhaps changing the approach, he can create a better outcome.

Let's Negotiate

"Everything is negotiable. Whether or not the negotiation is easy is another thing."—Carrie Fisher

As with our conversation about clarification, your ability to effectively negotiate your relationships depends upon the beliefs you have. Your beliefs about how relationships work, your role and responsibilities in them, what you say, and what you do all have beliefs that justify them.

The reason you shake hands when you meet someone is because you believe that is something important to do. The reason you make eye contact is because you believe it is important to make eye contact.

Let's begin discussing negotiation by defining it. How do you define *negotiation*? Some have described it as establishing give-and-take or common ground. Negotiation establishes agreements about the responsibilities of each person in the relationship. Some believe negotiation is about agreeing to what you're willing to give up in order to get what you want.

Take a moment to reflect upon your definition of negotiation, as it will shed light on your beliefs about it. Now let me offer you the first belief you must have before negotiation can even take place. The belief that "All relationships are negotiated." That means the people in relationships either verbally or nonverbally negotiate, or agree, how to relate to each other.

A negotiation in a relationship is an agreement about how to do "us". It is an agreement of the do's and don'ts of that relationship. Does that definition make sense to you?

I want you to think about this. It is a bit of a rhetorical question. Have you known someone who thinks, or have you thought of, negotiation as taking the necessary time to convince the other person how right you are? I have met many people like this.

They think that they have the most informed position on the matter and negotiation consists of being willing to hear them out so they can convince you of how wrong you are and how right they are.

In fact, if you think your job in a conversation is to wear somebody down into submission until he agrees... that is not negotiation. It's actually bullying.

When I point this out to people who do it, they are often surprised because they don't realize that is what they are doing—being so disrespectful to another person's point of view and right to be heard, and to offer his contribution to a conversation.

That is an important point to understand. It is only negotiation when the opinions and needs of both parties involved are respected and their needs are met as close to win-win as possible. If a person believes that relationships are based on win-lose, right or wrong, strength versus weakness, then they are competitive, not cooperative.

Do you feel that any of your relationships are competitive and feel like having an argument too much of the time?

If you'd like that to change, you need to start with your beliefs about your role in the relationship.

Nonverbal doesn't Help

"I think I'm constantly in a state of adjustment."—Patti Smith

Typically, if you can observe a person's nonverbal reactions to what you say and do, you can, then adjust how you relate to that person accordingly. This adjustment is an example of an unspoken negotiation. You don't even know you are doing it.

You just automatically watch the feedback and adjust, so you end up doing what the other person likes and avoid doing what the other person doesn't like.

Hopefully, she is paying attention to you and getting the same kind of feedback and making the same kind of adjustments. You both nonverbally negotiate what to do and not to do with each other.

However, if you miss that feedback, then you certainly can't use it to make the necessary adjustments.

When you are negotiating, it needs to be communicated in a more verbal and concrete way to be its most effective and, most importantly, so you can both be conscious of it.

Do I Have Common Sense?

"Common sense is not so common."—Voltaire

Don't you know that "It is common sense?" How many times have you been on the receiving end of that rhetorical question?

How do you feel when you're asked that question? Do you feel smarter, supported, or as though the person asking the question is taking an opportunity to call you stupid while claiming intellectual superiority?

Though I hear this concept of "common sense" batted around often, it occurred to me that this "common sense" can't be that common because the only time I seem to hear it mentioned is when someone is pointing out its absence.

How common can it be when so few people seem to have it?

So I reflected upon it and drew the following conclusion. Common sense exists in the mind of the beholder. As such, I feel that "common sense" can best be defined as the belief that your thoughts, habits, and routines are the correct ones and ought to be those of others as well.

I remember a week during my sophomore year in high school, during which I traveled with a friend and his family to spend some time on his older brother's farm in Wisconsin. I remember his brother trying to show me how to do something and when I couldn't figure it out he stated, "What are you, stupid or somethin'? This is common sense."

My point exactly, as a suburban boy like his younger brother, why would he expect me to know the intricate workings of his farm? His comment spoke more to his egocentrism than it did to my intelligence.

In our own daily lives in which we see ourselves as the center of the universe instead of an equal player in it, we can easily lose perspective.

This perspective can lead us to conclude that we know everything about how it's done and the world needs to take its cues from us. The alternative is to realize that we know very little and we best continue paying close attention to the new lessons that every person who enters our lives has to teach us.

Dealing with people who "Always" Want to Win

"There are two kinds of people: those who do the work and those who take the credit. Try to be in the first group; there is less competition there."—Indira Gandhi

Life is a competition, you either win or lose, succeed or fail, have power or weakness.

This is how people who always want to win see the world.

The biggest problem with this thinking is it makes working "with" others an illogical proposition.

Cooperation is seen as power sharing instead of combining strengths.

Making mistakes is experienced as an opening for attack from an adversary instead of an opportunity to utilize the strengths of others in accomplishing a win-win outcome.

You win when your needs get met, they win because they were able to be of value to you by contributing their gifts in helping you achieve a desired outcome. The win-win partnership is truly expressed when you do the same for them.

The choice to be offended

"Whenever anyone has offended me, I try to raise my soul so high that the offense cannot reach it."—Rene Descartes

A colleague of mine named Sarah Victory once said, "I think 10% of the people on the planet were put here just to be offended."

It's amazing how many of my fellow human beings seem to walk around looking for their buttons to be pushed.

Do you know anyone like this?

I know fewer and fewer of them as I exercise my ability to choose to keep my distance.

The fact is that choosing to be offended is often mistaken by people as an act of empowerment. "I found that remark to be offensive and I demand an apology."

The reality is that being offended is simply another reactive experience of life. It is the reaction of someone walking through life with the belief that their point of view is so special that it makes sense that others would agree with it.

When others don't, the reaction is SHOCK. "How dare you?" "Well, I never." And so on.

There was a time in my life when exposure to an idea outside my comfort zone might as well have been a declaration of war upon my self-declared moral authority. It's quite easy to spot those who have a similar reaction today.

What I eventually came to learn was what a slave I'd become to an inflexible ideology of "I'm right because I'm right." I'd made many decisions in my life that were so inflexible that I'd come to reject any opportunity to reflect upon them.

Times change, people change, people evolve and grow through the experience of new insights, new ideas and the opportunity to refine and reflect upon the decisions they've made about the world and their place in it.

It's not to say that reflection requires that you change your thinking, simply that you examine it in light of new information to be sure it still holds true for you, and for good reason.

The reason being is that it continues to produce the results in life that you want for yourself and those you love.

It's unfortunate to stick with the thinking you've always had, and insist on having, simply because it's familiar. Some of this thinking can become like an old pair of underwear you refuse to change simply because they feel so familiar to you. Get the point?

I don't have to agree with every new idea I'm exposed to, and there are many values such as kindness, compassion, and manners that stand the test of time.

So I enjoy the opportunities to reflect upon them, refine them, strengthen or replace them.

It's a hell of a lot more fulfilling than being offended by them.

Should I Build a Bridge or Burn One?

"Communication—the human connection—is the key to personal and career success."—Paul J. Meyer

Building relationships is no different than building a bridge. It takes time, a lot of thought, a lot of effort, and a lot of patience.

One morning, I watched part of a program about the construction of the Brooklyn Bridge and its designer, John Roebling. John was a brilliant but reclusive engineer. Getting the Brooklyn Bridge financed and built took 15 years and hundreds of meetings with toxic politicians and trustees who had their own agendas.

John didn't attend those meetings despite their demands; however, his wife, Emily, did. She was the one with the diplomacy skills, the confidence, and the determination to support her husband, the bridge, and the people who would ultimately build the bridge. Emily was known to visit the construction site and cheer up the workers. She was involved with the people at every level of the project.

One of Emily's greatest gifts, I suspect, and one of the keys to her effectiveness, was that she realized she wasn't building one bridge, she was building many.

A bridge is a connection between two things—pieces of land, or pieces of the heart. Emily was passionate about both. In order to make sure her husband John's vision was realized, she needed to build a bridge between herself, the politicians, the trustees, and the workers. She needed to connect with the hearts of those whose hearts needed to be invested over the 15 years it took to build the bridge, or it wouldn't have happened.

That same morning I saw my boys off to school. I hugged them, told them I loved them and I was proud of them. Those are two things I never want them to forget. Each time I tell them that I love them and that I'm proud of them, I am sending love across the bridge that connects our hearts.

Across the Brooklyn Bridge there is an endless stream, of cars, trucks, people, all bringing theirs joys and pains back and forth, back and forth. All day long.

When it comes to the bridges that connect us, we must be more deliberate with what we send across. Why would you send something to someone else's heart that you wouldn't want in your own? You wouldn't, would you?

In time, there are some bridges, which were once strong, that begin to fall apart because of poor maintenance. Sometimes because the quality of what is passed down the bridge diminishes.

A bridge that was once a passageway for love becomes a throughway for pain. That is when it is time to burn the bridge.

We do our utmost to pass along to others the best of ourselves through the bridges that connect our hearts. But, of course, bridges go two ways, back and forth.

When you consistently go forth and get only, or mostly, garbage back, it's time to burn the bridge.

Bridges take a long time to build, but a short time to burn.

Be mindful of what you send across and remember. If you don't want it in your own heart, don't put it in someone else's.

Do You Know What You're Doing?

"When a child is rescued, it sends the message that those helping doubt the child's abilities."—Brian R. King

How often have you been working diligently to learn something new only to have someone impatiently interrupt you with, "Do you know what you're doing?"

Even worse is when they rudely take the experience away from you with, "Let me do that. You clearly don't know what you're doing."

Actually, I do know what I'm doing... I'm learning. At least I was, until you decided I needed to get it right the first time, or on your timeline.

Have you ever done this to someone else?

What's that about for you?

Is it a need for control of the task, the situation, and the universe?

When was the decision made that the road to new knowledge and skill needed to be quick and smooth?

As someone with ADHD, Dyslexia and various other challenges I don't ever remember learning anything new easily. It took time, I took action, I got feedback, and I took new action until I found a way. That's learning. What I do remember is how amazing I felt each time I learned something new.

Please don't deny me, yourself, or anyone else that feeling of victory because you're too busy watching the clock. Life may be short but not so short that you can't support me in this moment. No matter how long it takes.

Advice That's Worth Ignoring

"The one thing people are the most liberal with, is their advice."—Francois de La Rochefoucauld

People care about you; people want to support you and often may want to advise you.

Simply receiving advice doesn't require you to take it. There's a question I strongly encourage clients to use to filter the advice they're given, "If I follow this person's advice, what results will I get?"

It is a human tendency to ask advice of people you trust but who aren't qualified to give you that advice.

You'd think the obvious would prevail but it often doesn't. There are people who are broke that also insist on giving friends and relatives financial advice.

People who only have jobs, don't own businesses and want to tell others how to run theirs.

A personal favorite: people who don't have children telling you how to raise yours.

The first people we tend to go to are those we trust, those we know care about us, and those more likely to tell us what we want to hear instead of what we need to hear.

They are also often unqualified to give us what we need to get the results we want. The best advice they can ever give us is advice on how to get the results they get.

So when you want to get different results than the results you're getting, you MUST find the people who actually get those results.

There's a saying that, "Opinions are like a**holes, everybody has one." The reality is that people have many opinions about many things, whether they are informed opinions or not.

In the end, they're all trying to help. In the end, you need to be very clear on the results you want to get before asking for advice from others.

Otherwise you'll end up with mediocre results because that's all the person you asked was qualified to teach you how to create.

Why Your Life is Only as Good as Who's in It

"The key is to keep company only with people who uplift you, whose presence calls forth your best."—Epictetus

When is the last time you took a good look at the people you surround yourself with?

If you examined each relationship, how would you answer this question: "In what way is my life better with this person in it?"

The bottom line is this: the quality of our lives is the sum total of the quality of our relationships. Surround yourself with lazy, negative, selfish people and you'll feel exhausted, frustrated, and like your needs don't matter.

But when you have people who are motivated, positive, loyal, and supportive in your life, it's amazing how you'll begin to adopt those same characteristics and begin to feel like thinking bigger and taking more risks to grow is a good idea.

But where do you find people like that? Good question. Here's the answer.

A recurring conversation I've had with my clients is how absolutely essential it is to form strategic partnerships.

A strategic partnership is a relationship in which you partner with another person who has a specific skill-set you lack and has agreed to support you in the areas of your life where their skills are useful. The most common examples are doctors, dentists, accountants, and mechanics to name a few.

The less known ones may be the friend who knows more about cars than you do and agrees to accompany you to the mechanic so you aren't taken advantage of.

Of course, before seeking out potential partners you need to know what help you need and be willing to ask for it.

Healthy candidates may be in your life right now; only you haven't been looking at them through the right lens.

In order to find the best person for each gap, it helps to have a sorting system to assist you in quickly determine who's the best fit and under what circumstances.

It is for this reason that I devised a five-category system I refer to as the Life Team Strategy™.

Keep in mind that these categories refer to attributes a person has and the quality of what that attribute brings to your life specifically. It isn't labeling the person's value as a human being but only refers to how well they fit your life and the direction you want to move in a specific situation.

Here's an important note: these categories can also apply to places and things, such as your beliefs. But for now, let's focus on how they apply to the people in your life.

When considering the attributes of a person, think about it in terms of your own skill set and whether this person's attributes are a good fit or a poor fit.

Ready?

1. Starters

Starters are your top-of-the-line strategic partners. They are the people you can count on to be there when you need them. If they say it, they do it. You can trust them, and when they help you, things get better. You must make it a priority in your life to surround yourself with these people, as they are the key to helping you grow and succeed in life.

2. Sneezers

Sneezers are the cheerleaders in your life. They are always offering encouragement, praising your accomplishments because they believe in you. They also speak well of you to others. They are great for a pep talk, but they are not in a position to run out onto the field and give you a hand like a Starter can.

3. Sitters

Sitters are inconsistent. They sit on the fence of life and you aren't sure at any given time when they're going to follow through.

4. Shovers

Shovers are the opposite of Starters. In a football game, they'd be the members of the other team. They want to succeed but have to make sure you don't in the process. Shovers act very deliberately to stand in your way. They are the physical bullies, the gossips, and the saboteurs who take specific action to trip you up.

At work, a Shover could be a coworker who's competing for the same promotion, or a supervisor who institutes unfair policy that makes your job more difficult. In a family, a Shover is most easily demonstrated by sibling rivalry or a spouse who refuses to work with you in parenting.

In terms of your thinking, if you hold two contradictory beliefs simultaneously, such as the desire to achieve goals, as well as the fear of failure, those beliefs are Shovers because they compete with each other and therefore prevent you from moving forward.

5. Shouters

Shouters are the fans and cheerleaders for the other team. They're the opposite of the Sneezers. A Shouter can be a person who says something with complete disregard for your feelings.

Shouters differ from Shovers in that they don't take direct action to stand in your way like a physical bully or a supervisor could because they don't have authority over you. A Shouter's strength is in messing with your head. A Shouter tells you that you're going to fall; the Shover actually trips you.

Shouters are the voices of doubt and negativity. They feel at their most competent when they can successfully talk you out of things that will likely improve your life. Unfortunately, Shouters are often the people who are closest to us.

A Shouter can often give you mixed messages of support and discouragement. For example, do you have people in your life who discourage you from thinking too big because they're afraid you'll be disappointed?

Is there someone you know who worries and always looks at the dark side of things? They tell you they worry because they love you and smother you, so that nothing bad happens to you. If these people and their thinking ever rub off on you, then they are contributing to your own self-doubt and negativity.

Shouters blame, criticize, and judge. You're being a Self-Shouter when you do these things to yourself.

The people in your life can play one, a few, or all of these roles at varying times. For example, someone who's successful in business but lousy in love could be a great Starter in terms of business advice, but would likely be a Shouter in terms of relationship advice.

It's also important to understand that you can switch roles on yourself as well. You may believe wholeheartedly in your abilities in one area and doubt yourself in another—going from Starter to Shouter.

I strongly encourage you to make a list of the Starters, Sneezers, Sitters, Shovers, or Shouters in your life. Also, make sure you list examples of the attributes that place them in that category.

Remember that each person can hold multiple positions in your life, depending on your needs. Someone may be a great Sneezer when you want encouragement but a Shover when you need a secret kept.

The power of making this list is that it allows you to be conscious of who you can count on in one instance and also where you need to avoid their input in another.

This is a heck of a foundation to get you started in assembling the Life Team that you need to finally get you headed in the direction you've always wanted to go, but didn't have the team to get you there. Here's to winning the championships! I'm happy to have been a Starter for you in this stage of your journey.

Why I Love Teachers

"One looks back with appreciation to the brilliant teachers, but with gratitude to those who touched our human feelings. The curriculum is so much necessary raw material, but warmth is the vital element for the growing plant and for the soul of the child."—Carl Jung

Who was your favorite teacher?

What was the most valuable lesson that he or she taught you?

For me, it was: I matter.

Who is the teacher that stands out in your mind for one important reason, because she made you feel like you stood out in hers?

It's increasingly difficult nowadays, with government mandates that seem to think success is measured more by tests than creativity and innovation, to help a child learn and celebrate the things that make him shine. But it is still possible.

I slipped through the cracks more often than not, seldom got the support I needed, was bullied mercilessly at times and could have easily curled up in a corner and given up.

But while it felt like no one cared whether I lived or died much of the time, there was a select group of people throughout my life who took notice. Who took the time and made the effort to see to it that I knew I mattered.

Who were these people? Teachers.

In third grade, my art teacher Mrs. Zahaitis saw that I was very self-critical and how I often quit before I even started. She was the first to identify me as "my own worst enemy". She was right, and she never gave up on me. I remember her calm demeanor and her patience as she helped me find my way through the various art projects.

I don't remember any of the art projects and am not particularly interested in art. What I remember was the relationship.

Now I see my son Aidan light up when it's art class day at school. He has an artistic talent I never had and am thrilled that he has the experience of being nurtured in that way.

In sixth grade, there was Miss Gallagher. I had her for music class but at some point she noticed I was dabbling in poetry. She read every poem I wrote as though it were the most magnificent thing ever written. It wasn't that she was giving me inflating praise, what she was doing was encouraging me to continue and refine what I was writing. Look how far I've come.

In seventh and eighth grade, there was Mrs. Clarke. She was my counselor and very much a teacher. She never asked me to go any faster than I needed to, to make things work. Whenever I'd take one step forward and five steps back, she was there to understand, validate my frustrations, and help me move forward again.

Then, there's the greatest teacher I ever had. I was lost through my first two years of high school until in my junior year when I met Mrs. Aronoff. I didn't have her as a classroom teacher; instead she was the faculty advisor for a group I was in that focused on bringing drug abuse awareness programs to the grade schools.

This group was my first exposure to public service and Mrs. Aronoff saw abilities in me that she was compelled to nurture. She was my greatest mentor and now 20 + years since high school graduation, she has become a trusted friend.

She retired this past school year and we had a conversation by phone in which I told her of all the ways she contributed to the person I've become. Most of all, I made it very clear to her, that when she looks back at her legacy as a teacher, she can think of me.

The greatest lesson I learned from each of these amazing teachers was that I had more to offer them than just my undivided attention. Sure, there are teachers who seemed rushed and more focused on completing tasks than relating to their students.

Then, there are those that who realize the power of their relationships with their students. I've benefited from it; my two older sons are now benefiting from it. And I always smile when I hear stories from clients of their experiences with those who truly get it.

Teachers are some of the most phenomenal multi-taskers in the world. All while they work long hours, for less money than they're worth, and often receive far more criticism than they ever deserve.

They continue each and every day to show up and work their butts off in the hope that they can help the student who just needs that opportunity to shine.

Who was your favorite teacher?

What was the most valuable lesson that he taught you?

Everyone's a Role model

"Before you decide to have children, ask yourself this question: 'Would I want my child to learn to be the person I am now?' The person you are now is the role model they're going to have."
—Brian R. King

The #1 question I ask my clients to help build their self-awareness is something I simply call the Role Model Question. Let's start by defining what it means to be a Role Model. My definition of a Role Model is someone who through his or her actions demonstrates how to do something effectively. This can be as broad as how to succeed in a career, a task, or as specific as a single character trait.

Too many people think self-awareness means you have to look at yourself with an eye on criticism. Self-awareness simply means you're paying attention. You're simply watching your thoughts and decisions to better understand the results you create. The better you understand, the more precisely you can determine where to refine your efforts to get different results.

Here's the Role Model Question: "If the people of the world were watching you live your life as an example for how to live theirs, what would they learn from your example?"

You can answer this question with the words you use, the choices you make, and the actions you take. The point isn't to judge the answers you give, the point is to reflect upon

240

them to determine if what you're modeling is the person you truly are and truly want to be.

So many people are shocked by the degree to which they deceive themselves. The degree to which they model things like, "How to pretend you're happy when you're not", "How to lie convincingly", or "How to let someone take advantage you".'" We know many people who model hypocrisy, but do we acknowledge the times when *we* model it? The list goes on and on.

I ask myself this question frequently as a self-awareness check. At any given time, I may be modeling compassion, patience, tenacity, resilience, loyalty, while other times I'm modeling self-criticism, how to take things personally, and how to worry.

Overall, based on my own reflection and the feedback of others, traits I consistently model are imperfection, vulnerability, and perseverance. In other words, I model my humanity. I model exactly who I am, warts and all.

So why leave myself so open in this way? Have I learned this from others? Not quite. We live in a world where our leaders won't share their vulnerability, where they blame others for what isn't working and pretend to be larger than life.

Those closest to us and those who employ us may practice a "do as I say not as I do" philosophy.

I learned to be myself more and more over time as I went through the process of healing some deep emotional pain. I learned that the only way to heal pain is to feel it and work through it. Only then can you get past it.

I've been pleasantly surprised by those who express gratitude to me for being willing to bear my soul in this way. They explain how dangerous they've found doing so in their own lives because of those who take advantage of their vulnerable moments. I say shame on those for modeling how to exploit others and how to knock them down instead of lifting them up.

So where do we find the role models we want and need in a world where hypocrisy seems so abundant? The question to answer first is, what do you want to learn? Do you want to learn how to shoot a free throw, or do you want to learn patience?

Would you like to surround yourself with those who feel they're better than everyone else or with those committed to being in service of others? Once you decide what you want to do or be, you can begin looking for the person who not only exemplifies that trait or skill, but also gets the results you're looking to create with that trait or ability.

Well, what if you don't know what you want? Do you tend to say one thing and do another? Do you say you want to accomplish something and do everything to sabotage success?

What do you do then?

Let's use the Role Model question. Say you're prolific at procrastinating and making excuses. I had a client like this who, upon reflection, admitted to his procrastination, laziness, and avoidance. My next question to him was: "As a role model, your job is to demonstrate to the person looking up to you that your life style is the way to go. How do you do that?"

He was unable to defend his lifestyle, let alone want to sell anyone on it. That opened the door to discussing whether how he chose to live his life helped him accomplish his goals in any way.

What he determined was that the life he lived was more in service of meeting the needs of the moment, instead of working towards anything long term. As such, he realized his needs were to avoid boredom and responsibility.

What next?

I asked him what traits he wanted to model, if not the ones he currently practiced? At first, he was unsure. I asked him what problems he would need to solve in order to get his needs met. Needs, as simple as food, shelter, and clothing require certain skill sets in order to get those needs met.

We determined that he needed skills, such as organization and proactivity, to plan and cook a meal. His shelter was provided for him, but he could begin by learning to participate in its upkeep.

A character trait such as service-mindedness, and cooperativeness, comes into play in asking how he can help around the house. Organization is needed again in planning his day to include the tasks he wishes to complete, the order to complete them, and the time he wishes to complete them. Self-discipline is examined and developed as he determines how well he follows through.

Once you've determined what traits or skills you want to learn, then you can ask yourself, "Who do I know who I can learn this from?" If you don't, ask around until you find that person. Then you watch, listen, learn, and duplicate. Easier said than done, I know, but that is my formula. Connecting with this person requires a skill set in its own right.

Let's finish with this. I encourage you to ask yourself these questions.

Who do I model?

What characteristics/actions about them do I model?

Why do I model that?

What results do I get?

What does this say about my values?

Is what I choose to model something I want to have modeled back to me?

If not, what action am I prepared to take, to address it?

Work Together instead of Falling Apart

"Communication: the thing humans forgot when we invented words."—Richard Branson

People, in general, are very good at continuing to do the things that don't work in relationships, even when those things cause pain.

One of the biggest challenges in many relationships stems from a desire to do for one another or to compete with each other. What they seem unable to do is to work together.

Do you know anyone with this issue, either ongoing or occasional?

What I have found is that there are specific habits that occur in relationships that result in division. Fortunately, each habit has a counterpart that creates collaboration. Therefore I'll present them together to make discussing them easier.

The key is to know what they are, when you're using a division strategy, then quickly using the strategy that will restore collaboration. Got it?

Responsibility versus Blame

"One's philosophy is not best expressed in words; it is expressed in the choices one makes... and the choices we make are ultimately our responsibility."—Eleanor Roosevelt

Responsibility. Now there's a familiar term. Responsibility is the ability to respond to life's events in a proactive way. It requires you to take complete ownership of your decisions and your actions ahead of time and after the fact.

What is blame? It is assigning responsibility, particularly for wrong-doing on the part of someone or something else. It results from the decision that you've been victimized in some way, that power has been taken from you.

Zach, my 15-year-old son, was the consummate blamer for years. He would tease his brothers whenever he was bored and say he couldn't help it. Whenever roughhousing would go bad, he'd defend himself by saying, "He started it."

He seemingly took responsibility for nothing.

So, in order to help him understand what he was doing, I modeled the very same behavior.

For example, on one occasion we were running errands. Zach sat in the car for a few minutes while I did a quick in and out.

When I came back and slid into the driver's seat I lightly slugged him on the arm. He said, "What did you do that for?" I said, "I don't know, I just couldn't help myself. You were sitting right there, you were just asking for it. I had to do it."

He says, "What are you talking about? I didn't do anything."
I said, "Well, maybe you didn't, but in this family, we blame each other for our actions, right, isn't that the rule?"

He responded with a smirk.

He learned quickly that whenever he chose to blame, I'd decide to follow that rule for myself as well.

When on the receiving end of it, it made a lot more sense to him than a lecture as to why blaming wasn't logical. Experience is a much better teacher.

Overall, people who blame, as a defense, an explanation, or a way to deflect responsibility, don't realize to what degree they're disempowering themselves. In a moment where they can be empowered, they instead choose helplessness. That's what blame does.

Accepting responsibility is a claim of power in the situation.

Now, when I say power, I don't mean force. By power, I mean that inherent ability to take action to create results. It's exercising your ability to choose your response, instead of simply having a reaction.

In what aspects of your life do you accept responsibility?

By accepting responsibility you are taking charge of learning and applying the knowledge and skills required to create the results you want.

Now, are there aspects of your life in which you exercise blame? If so, what things do you blame? What people do you blame?

Do you blame your parents? The weather? Your age?

We could probably talk for hours on that. What do you blame your parents for?

If you blame your parents for the way they raised you, at what point do you accept responsibility for continuing to follow their lead instead of improving upon it?

It's about making choices.

There's an old saying: "For the way you turned out, shame on your parents. If you stay that way, shame on you."

There must come a point when you examine any divisive relationship habit you're practicing regardless of where you learned it. Then, in that moment of clarity, say to yourself, "I don't like the results I'm getting—there must be a better way than this." Then open your mind a little wider and begin looking for new role models.

How do you know when you have the right role models for you?

You like the results you're getting! Happiness is a wonderful way of knowing that you're on the right track.

I was a big-time blamer, my own worst enemy for a large part of my life. I could turn anything into a negative.

If someone said, "Oh it's a bright, sun-shiny day." I'd say, "Just wait." But at some point I experienced the moment of clarity, when I realized I didn't like the results I was getting and needed to turn things around.

Responsibility, especially in a partnership, is an agreement to take action together to combine your efforts, combine your gifts, to create a desired result.

Proactivity versus procrastination

"Procrastination is the bad habit of putting off until the day after tomorrow what should have been done the day before yesterday."
—Napoleon Hill

Procrastination is something we're all familiar with and for some of us it's an absolutely paralyzing habit. One we say repeatedly we need to do something about, and yet... we put that off, too. So what gives?

So why do we procrastinate? Is it due to a lack of motivation? On the contrary, procrastination is driven by motivation. In fact, I define procrastination as the motivation to avoid. Avoid what? Avoid pain, that's what.

We put off the tasks, experiences, etc., that we believe will cause us pain if we take action on them. We then, of course, associate prolonged pleasure in delaying action.

So how do you shift this pattern once and for all, so you can replace procrastination with proactivity and feel more empowered than fearful?

Begin by identifying your Procrastination story. This is the story you tell yourself about why taking action will result in pain, frustration, boredom, or any other experience you want to avoid.

Your story is what is kicking your butt and NOT the task itself. Identify the key variables in your story—your beliefs in the form of: "If I do _____, then _____ will happen."

Here's the awesome part. Ready?

It's your story, so you can rewrite it. Change out the variables so the story you tell yourself focuses on positive outcomes that can only be experienced by taking action, instead of the present form in which you focus on painful problems that could occur.

In short...

The power lies in being the author of the beautiful story that is your life. As any successful author will tell you, the most important writing skill to master is the art of rewriting.

Feedback versus criticism

"Feedback is the breakfast of champions."—Ken Blanchard

What's the difference?

Criticism is a judgment in which what took place was not good enough. Feedback is just giving information.

A key element to differentiate the two is permission. When someone wants to give you his two cents and you didn't ask for it, it's typically heard as criticism.

When she asks for your input on something because she wants to improve it, that's feedback. Make sense?

Feedback begins with an agreement to give each other information about what's working and not working.

When you can get into the habit of giving each other feedback in a supportive way and receiving it with gratitude, it creates a foundation for discussing the very difficult things in your relationships.

Compassion versus pity

"Our human compassion binds us the one to the other—not in pity or patronizingly, but as human beings who have learnt how to turn our common suffering into hope for the future."—Nelson Mandela

What does compassion mean to you?

Compassion, in my experience, is that sense of being able to look at any other human being and say to yourself, we share this experience called the human journey. We're in this together. There's more about us that is alike than dissimilar.

One of the things that we tend to have compassion for is the suffering we see in others. You know why? Because we get it, we can relate to that.

Pity is when you think you're better than the person who is suffering.

Compassion comes from a place of deep respect for that person's humanity. What allows your compassion to benefit somebody else is the understanding that he's in a place that you can relate to, because you were there at one point.

Maybe you're not there right now. Maybe you're in a more resourceful place and now by reaching out to him with compassion, you can invite him to join you in the place you're at.

Ignorance is at the heart of pity. When you only know your own experience and believe it is the default experience of life, your subjectivity, when things are going well, creates the feeling that everybody else's life must really suck.

There are some people who are like that, unfortunately. They think that their life is perfect or better, and some of that might be a rationalization, some of that might be an honest assessment.

Compassion realizes that we're all fellow travelers here; we're all in it together. We have more experiences alike than different.

Two words, that are a constant reminder of just how alike and connected we are, are the words "Me, too."

Those words are a powerful reminder that we're in it together.

Permission versus imposition

"Do not impose on others what you yourself do not desire."
—Confucius

Who has the choice in permission?

Someone who invites you to contribute to her life is giving you permission to do so.

Imposition occurs when you feel entitled to it and therefore impose yourself upon her.

An issue I had with my own mother at one point was her feeling entitled to displays of affection from my sons.

She would demand hugs and kisses and then lay a guilt trip on the son who wouldn't oblige her.

The final straw came on one occasion when I saw her guilt trip my youngest into feeling that he had wronged her somehow and he ended up hugging her even though he didn't want to.

I asked my wife to escort him out of the room, as I probably in less than good form, and I informed my mother what the rule was. That it is his body, it is his right, it is up to him to give permission to whomever he chooses to allow them into his space.

He can deny me the right to give him a hug and he often does and "Good for him!" Because if I don't teach him that value—if I teach him he is obligated to give physical affection to adults—who's going to exploit that? Pedophiles and a lot of adults don't realize that.

Teach kids at a very young age that their body is sacred. They give you permission to come into their space. And permission giving—asking permission for anything, is a significant sign of respect to give a person.

Imposition is when you feel that you have the right to do something because you know better for somebody else... you're smarter than they are, and they have no say in the matter.

There's one exception that trumps everything and that's safety. You don't take the time to ask, "Do I have your permission to pull you out of the street before this car hits you?" You just do it.

Forgiveness versus guilt

"Forgiveness is not always easy. At times, it feels more painful than the wound we suffered, to forgive the one that inflicted it. And yet, there is no peace without forgiveness."—Marianne Williamson

One of the biggest saboteurs of forgiveness is called scorekeeping. It occurs when one, or both partners is silently keeping track of every infraction the other has committed. Then, whenever she brings an infraction to his attention, he'll respond by saying, "Oh yeah? Well, what about the time you did this, or, you know, the time you did that?" Then he'll unleash with his cumulative list of all the things you did wrong that make what he did pale by comparison.

He does this to try and make her feel guilty for all the wrongs that she's done, so he doesn't have to take responsibility for what they did. Guilt is, unfortunately, a commonly used very toxic tool in relationships. The healing side of which is forgiveness.

So how do you become proficient at forgiving?

It can be very difficult when you feel a particular action is unforgivable.

Is it a matter of simply deciding to put your energies elsewhere?

A powerful aspect of forgiveness is the compassion we were discussing earlier. Compassion, when you consider that we each have those human moments where we fail to live from the best parts of ourselves.

There may be times when another chance is warranted. There may be times when you've given multiple chances and now it's time to walk away. In both cases, forgiveness is what allows you to move past the event instead of dragging it behind you.

So if you want that for yourself, you better darn well extend it. Forgiveness is the understanding that we all blow it from time to time. I can let it go, I can let you try again, and sometimes I must let you go.

A lesson from my own life came when my oldest son Zach was in first grade. He was bullied by staff and other students who didn't understand him and wouldn't work with him.

I ended up homeschooling him and there was a time I hated those I felt did him wrong and I let everyone know it. I wanted them all fired; I couldn't say anything nice about them. I didn't want to forgive them because what they did was cold and unprofessional.

I told myself a story about why they shouldn't be forgiven. At some point, I realized what this was doing to Zach. He couldn't move beyond it and heal because I wouldn't.

I realized what I needed to do for him was reframe it so he could understand how far he'd come since then. It was an opportunity to learn to be resilient, a time to draw strength from, and a learning opportunity.

I had to reframe it for myself as an opportunity instead of proof that life was unfair.

Service versus selfishness

"To give real service you must add something which cannot be bought or measured with money, and that is sincerity and integrity." - Douglas Adams

Is your focus on me at the expense of "We"?

Clarification versus assumption

"Question everything. Learn something. Answer nothing."
—Euripides

Assumption is expecting your partner to read your mind instead of asking for what you need. Then blaming your partner for their lack of superpowers.

Gratitude versus entitlement

"No one who achieves success does so without acknowledging the help of others. The wise and confident acknowledge this help with gratitude."—Alfred North Whitehead

Gratitude stems from understanding that nobody owes you a darn thing, that we are intimately connected and interdependent with one another. You are therefore grateful for everything anybody extends into your life.

Growth versus stubbornness

"In my early professional years I was asking the question: How can I treat, or cure, or change this person? Now I would phrase the question in this way: How can I provide a relationship which this person may use for his own personal growth?"—Carl Rogers

In relationships, if you are not with somebody who is helping you grow, you're either with the wrong person or you're in the wrong place. Stubbornness is all about hanging on; it's about the desire to be right, over the desire to be happy.

Stubbornness is about meeting your own needs. Growth is about seeing to it that the other person you've committed your life to is making progress, and that this person is helping you make progress as well.

When you realize growth is the name of the game, you'll want to give the people who give you permission to enter their lives the very best of yourself, whenever possible.

Keep in mind that these ten habits are the tip of the iceberg. They are guidelines to help you be more conscious of what you can choose to bring to any partnership.

When you do show up in a partnership, what are you going to do to enhance connection, connection of things that bring you together, to put you on the same page, create those experiences of "me too"?

Those opportunities to share compassion, to be in it together, to grow with one another, as opposed to pointing fingers, procrastinating, assigning blame, feeling pity, and anything else that prevents the two of you from coming together.

You will always be in it together—the question is whether you'll do whatever it takes to come together.

Discussion Questions

One of the ways we learn is through dialogue. I, for one, learn best when discussing ideas with others. This book was a discussion about ways we create perfect moments in our lives.

Below are a series of questions inspired by the content of this book. Questions you can use as the basis of discussion with friends, family or colleagues. I hope you find them helpful in expanding the value of the lessons found throughout this book. Feel free to record your answers in a journal, as well.

What are the qualities/characteristics of perfect moments?

How are responsibility, resourcefulness, resilience, and reciprocity related? Can you have one of those without another? Do you think one trait is developed before another? If so, which one? Or, do you think they are all developed simultaneously?

What's the difference between responsibility and blame? How can you learn to take responsibility instead of blaming others or giving excuses (see *Responsibility*)?

Brian shares in the passage titled *Reciprocity*, "My strengths are the reason you need me and my challenges are the reason I need you." What are your strengths? How can they benefit and make a difference in your children/students? What are some of the biggest challenges that you face from your relationships? How can your strengths benefit and help them to improve their challenges? Now, flipping that around, what are your biggest challenges? How can your relationships help you with your challenges?

"Practice makes perfect." But, as Brian points out, what are you practicing? If you were to take note of the traits in your life you'd like to change, can you find the other behaviors you are doing that support those same negative traits? What can you practice more of in your life (see *Your First Thought of the Day*)?

In *Stop Pushing my Buttons*, Brian shares a formula and some questions to ask yourself when you find yourself upset. It's certainly easy to talk about ways to make tense moments better before they happen. But what can you do to help yourself remember these steps and ask yourself these questions while you are in the heat of the moment?

Are you accepting of other people's opinion even if you absolutely don't agree?

Do you have the ability to see someone's opinion if you disagree with it?

When you look back at your life, think of a person who supported you through a difficult period. Have you expressed gratitude to that person?

Have you ever asked for feedback on an area of your life in which you could improve? Why or why not?

Do you have toxic people in your life? If yes, why are they still in your life?

How will you know when it's time to burn a bridge between yourself and another person?

What would your life look like without that person in it?

How do you answer a question when you do not know the answer?

When upset over something that was said to you, do you clarify with the person involved to see if you understood what they said correctly, or to verify that your feelings are valid?

Do you agree that asking questions, no matter how stupid *you think* the question is, can be a learning experience for both the person asking the question and the person being asked?

As a teacher or parent, do you talk honestly to the class or your children about a disability, disease, and/or condition that someone in the class has, your child has, or maybe you have? If not, why?

Think about a relationship you've had in the past that was painful in many ways and eventually ended. Are you able to reflect upon it and find lessons for which you are grateful?

When was the last time you praised someone? What happened?

Do you graciously accept help from others when needed?

Do you, in turn, pay it forward to help others? Do you model this for others? If so, how?

Do you encourage others to do something new, even if you know they can't do it or will likely struggle? Why?

Who would you need to be in order to keep "swinging" when your efforts seem to not be paying off they way you would like?

What does it feel like to you when someone gives you his or her undivided attention?

Have you experienced a time in life when you were more dependent on others? For example, surgery, broken bone, etc. How did you manage that time mentally and emotionally? Why?

What is one characteristic you have that someone may consider you to be a role model for that characteristic?

What is the one trait you would like to model more effectively?

What are the pros and cons of using social media as a means of building your relationships?

Of the six treasures of friendship, which one is your best quality as a friend?

Of the six treasures of friendship, which one is a quality you need to improve?

Series Note:

I hope you enjoyed our journey together. I would be humbled and grateful if you thought enough of this book to refer it to others.

It is also with great pleasure that I invite you to continue this journey with me. This book is the first in a series of Perfect Moments in Relationships titles. Future books in the series will focus on specific aspects of life such as parenting, marriage, friendship and more.

I hope you'll consider sharing your best stories of the perfect moments of your life with me, so I can, in turn, share them with the world.

Please visit my website, http://BrianRaymondKing.com, for all the details on how your story can become a part of the Perfect Moments in Relationships series.

ABOUT THE AUTHOR

Brian R. King LCSW is a 25-year cancer survivor, adult with Dyslexia, ADHD, and Asperger's. He's also the father of three sons on the autism spectrum. He is known worldwide for his books and highly engaging presentations that teach the power of connection and collaboration. His strategies empower others to overcome their differences, so they can build powerful and lasting partnerships. His motto is: We're all in this together.

More information about Brian's books, coaching, and presentations can be found at http://BrianRaymondKing.com

www.ingramcontent.com/pod-product-compliance
Lightning Source LLC
Chambersburg PA
CBHW031502270326
41930CB00006B/217